"In a time of unrest and chaos, Helen's story of her amazing journey as an American immigrant is a light to those seeking a better life. She brings you into her life with all its sacrifice, hope, and personal development. Reading about it is like listening to your best friend share their most intimate feelings on the events of their life. It is an absolute inspiration for everyone to see that one can accomplish almost anything if they are committed to it. Her commitment to be something more than expected has you rooting for her to succeed, and the horrors of the journey will bring tears. One can't help but feel better and be inspired to do more after reading her story. Almost a 'how to' manual on how to immigrate and succeed in the United States."

—Eric Rehn, CCIM, 2017 president of NorCal CCIM

"Helen is the hardest working person we know. We met her about ten years ago, and since then she has grown from a residential agent to an expert in both residential and commercial real estate. She always gives her 100 percent for all tasks, and her efforts helped grow our portfolio significantly.

Her humble beginnings in Indonesia taught her a good work ethic and perseverance. She took advantage of crises and made them into opportunities. She is a great example of achieving the American Dream. All real estate investors or working women can learn key lessons from reading her book."

—Winnie Liu, CPA, CFA, MBA, real estate investor; Thomas Liu, MD, PhD, orthopedic surgeon

"*Helen Chong's book,* Power to Change Lives, *is a candid depiction of how some of the greatest obstacles in life can not only be overcome, but can result in growth. Helen's unfettered description of her life and the lessons she learned—from her determination to step outside what was expected of her and follow her own dreams, to dealing with the never-spoken-about realities of pregnancy and post-partum life—are both moving and relatable. As women in a leadership roles, or as women in general, exposing our vulnerabilities and our imperfections and admitting that life is not always sunshine and roses is not easy. Helen shares these very personal moments with us in a way that lets us know that it is okay to be all of these—imperfect, vulnerable, and challenged—and that by embracing the imperfections, vulnerabilities, and challenges in our lives, we can take those lessons and become stronger, wiser, and more successful.*"

The views expressed are those of the author and do not reflect the official policy or position of the US Navy, Department of Defense, or the US Government.

—Ana Tempone, Commander, US Navy

"Power to Change Lives *will not only inspire you; it will give you incredible insight into what it takes to adapt and thrive through significant changes, both in life and in business. Helen Chong's story challenges us to find the resiliency and power within ourselves and apply that in pursuit of our ambitions and dreams. It is not very often that you encounter someone that has actualized 'the American Dream,' but Helen embodies that in a way that is vivid and picturesque. If you are someone who is looking for inspiration and the resolve to pursue your aspirations,* Power to Change Lives *is a must-read.*"

—Guy Gal, founder and CEO, Side Inc.

"In her captivating and evocative first book, Power To Change Lives, *Helen Chong aims to tell 'the full story' of what it means to be an immigrant student in America, in all of its fraught complexity. She gives a candid and comprehensive account of how to succeed in real estate investment and achieve financial success."*

—Sanjeev Jaiswal, CEO, iFiber Optix Inc.

*"*Power to Change Lives *is truly an inspiration to anyone who has achieved incredible success and wealth after being faced with adversity, racism, and cultural differences. As a business and life coach, I am often reading and recommending leadership stories of perseverance and success, but the story that the author portrays in this book is truly incredible! Helen Chong shares with her readers a front-line tale about one young woman's journey into a new country, learning a new language, and eventually pushing herself to become one of the top authorities on real estate investing in the United States. Her dedication to her family motivates her along the way, but the true grit and determination that this young Chinese girl takes on to make a name for herself make this a book any aspiring immigrant should read. Her grind is nonstop! I would recommend this to any young woman who is looking to break through traditional stereotypes to make a name for herself as her own CEO against insurmountable odds."*

—Andi Cummings, owner and coach, Platinum Coaching Group

*"*Power to Change Lives *is beyond counterfeit! A real person can do extraordinary things. Helen's story truly embodies the American Dream."*

—Dan Higgison, founder and CEO, Synergy Worldwide

"Helen's journey of perseverance and self-improvement to expand her boundaries and chart her own career path is inspiring; her willingness to share the vulnerable moments along the way make her success that much richer for the reader."

—Croft Young, investment banker

POWER TO
CHANGE LIVES

HELEN CHONG

POWER TO CHANGE LIVES

HOW TO LEVERAGE LIFE'S OBSTACLES TO REACH FINANCIAL SUCCESS

Published by Advantage, Charleston, South Carolina.
Member of Advantage Media Group.

ADVANTAGE is a registered trademark, and the Advantage colophon is a trademark of Advantage Media Group, Inc.

Printed in the United States of America.

10 9 8 7 6 5 4 3 2 1

ISBN: 978-1-64225-069-5
LCCN: 2020924101

Cover design by David Taylor.
Layout design by Mary Hamilton.

This publication is designed to provide accurate and authoritative information in regard to the subject matter covered. It is sold with the understanding that the publisher is not engaged in rendering legal, accounting, or other professional services. If legal advice or other expert assistance is required, the services of a competent professional person should be sought.

Advantage Media Group is proud to be a part of the Tree Neutral® program. Tree Neutral offsets the number of trees consumed in the production and printing of this book by taking proactive steps such as planting trees in direct proportion to the number of trees used to print books. To learn more about Tree Neutral, please visit **www.treeneutral.com**.

Advantage Media Group is a publisher of business, self-improvement, and professional development books and online learning. We help entrepreneurs, business leaders, and professionals share their Stories, Passion, and Knowledge to help others Learn & Grow. Do you have a manuscript or book idea that you would like us to consider for publishing? Please visit **advantagefamily.com** or call **1.866.775.1696**.

To my parents, Lenny and Yung Ming, who reminded me of the importance of maintaining a strong and honorable character even during adversity.

CONTENTS

Mother, how are you today?
Here is a note from your daughter
With me everything is okay
Mother, how are you today?

—*Maywood, "Mother How Are You Today?"*

INTRODUCTION

A home is more than a structure; it's a universal symbol of family, comfort, and security. Our first home is our mother's womb, and from a collective standpoint, we are all on a journey to rediscover that peace again. Even the animal world organizes itself around the instinctive drive to find nests, burrows, hollows, and caves. This innate impulse to find a place of security where we belong is a vital part of the human experience and is perhaps why homecomings are common themes in epic poems and heroic quests.

Though I didn't set out to write an odyssey, I suppose in some ways that's exactly what I did—my story, spanning decades and continents, intermingles heroes and villains and explores the ways seemingly superhuman forces shape their universe. In my early years, it seemed conflict followed me and yearning guided me. I now understand that the interplay of conflict and yearning helped give rise to the power to change my mindset, which propelled me toward my future successes.

Over the last fifteen years, I have negotiated millions of dollars of real estate transactions and grossed hundreds of millions of dollars in equity for my clients. I understand that homes are sacred spaces that house personal histories, and they can have great impacts on our lives. Whether we are aware of it or not, home buying is bigger than the purchase of a structure: it's a return to something sacred that we've longed for. Home buying actualizes the symbol of *home,* taking it from a mental construct to a physical reality. Owning a home alters something within us and gives us places to build memories and be wholly ourselves.

I started writing a book so that my children would understand how their mother, who grew up poor on the other side of the world, came to the United States, built a career for herself through her own hard work and determination, and created for them a life unlike any she herself had ever known. In the last several years, I've garnered speaking opportunities that have given me platforms to share parts of my story. It was the feedback from these occasions that made me realize that humans are wired for connection. Stories provide us paths toward empowerment, validation, and communion, no matter our current challenges. Not only did I need to share my experiences with my children, but I also needed to share them with anyone who feels as lost as I once did.

We are all guilty of projecting cultivated personas. In our social media culture, it's easier than ever to only show the shiny, happy sides of ourselves. I do not think this is honest, nor do I think it helps people feel connected. In these pages, I will reveal the ugly truth— that the path to success is sometimes dark, lonely, and scary. Using my own experience of leaving home and the ensuing decades-long journey to find my way back, I share the struggles and disadvantages that threatened to ensnare me as a poor, minority, female immigrant. We need to hear people's authentic tales of strife so that we have guides along our own journeys. Without those guides, we may never get to our destinations.

This book will interweave my own experiences with the lessons I have learned along the way about business, life, balance, growth, and wealth building. I want to share what I know about goal setting and perseverance and how those tools can benefit you on your own personal and professional paths. I share advice on creating financial well-being, but as I have discovered on my own journey, there are greater rewards like happiness, freedom, and choice. This book is meant to inspire people who feel like they have no resources and no hope. Trust me, you can be successful. Using the steps and lessons I outline throughout the following chapters, you too can find your way back home—a place of safety, security, and eternal belonging.

CHAPTER ONE

CHILDHOOD MEMORIES OF HOME

n my career, I often find myself debating with clients and friends about the benefits of renting a home versus buying a home. As a real estate broker and investor, I have a number of tangible reasons why buying a home is a sound long-term financial investment, but the major reason I feel so strongly about buying a home is intangible. In fact, it's quite personal.

When my husband and I bought our first home in 2013, we had two children with a third on the way. We had moved seven times in the previous four years, and the joke had become that with each pregnancy, we moved into a new house. It seemed I took nesting to a new level! After renting for several years, and paying a 7 percent increase each year, I didn't want *any* nest; I wanted my *own* nest.

On moving day, I felt immense pride. I told my three-year-old and one-year-old children, "This is the home you'll remember for the rest of your lives." From that first day, my children excitedly ran around their new backyard. Not much has changed in the last five years, except now there are three children zooming up and down the hallway and scooting out into the yard during their frequent playdates. This is what I want them to remember—the sweet chaos of weekends spent playing with their siblings and friends in a home of their own, the dinners together around our family table, the sunny days spent exploring and imagining the wide world from the safety of their own backyard.

It's not just my children who have benefited from the purchase of our home—my husband and I have felt more settled and stable as well. I have watched all areas of my life improve after the purchase of my home. The solid foundation it provides has allowed me to take professional risks and has accelerated my career in ways not often associated with homeownership. I feel I'm building something from this house. I feel grounded and emboldened. My children feel this too. With my family happy and my career expanding, I feel peace.

> I SPEND MY DAYS HELPING OTHERS FIND THEIR OWN WAYS BACK HOME. WHETHER THEY ARE SEEKING A LARGE HOME OR A SMALL HOME, THE POWER LIES IN WHAT THE HOME CAN PROVIDE THEM: SAFETY, COMFORT, FREEDOM, A FIXED FOUNDATION.

I spend my days helping others find their own ways back home. Whether they are seeking a large home or a small home, the power lies in what the home can provide them: safety, comfort, freedom, a fixed foundation. I'm learning to be grateful every day for the arduous path that led me home. Despite the contentment of today, however, I often wish I could go back to eighteen-year-old me—scared, poor, and living alone in this foreign country—and tell her, "Don't worry, you will find your way home."

GROWING UP IN HONG KONG

I remember waking in the middle of the night in our rental home in Hong Kong and hearing my parents working in the spare room that was filled with boxes and packaging materials. I'd wander in sleepy-eyed, and my parents would shoo me away: "Go back to sleep." At the time, I didn't understand why they would rush me back to sleep, but now I understand that they needed this time to work. Without their constant willingness to labor hard and their unwavering dedication to their work ethic, we would not have had a home of our own. Seeing their hard work stayed with me

> YOU WORK HARD SO THAT YOU CAN PROVIDE FOR YOUR FAMILY, AND SOMETIMES IN PROVIDING THEM WITH MATERIAL THINGS, YOU'RE ACTUALLY PROVIDING THEM WITH THINGS OF EVEN GREATER VALUE—LIKE RESPITE, SECURITY, PEACE.

as I grew older. I understood that you work hard so that you can provide for your family, and sometimes in providing them with material things, you're actually providing them with things of even greater value—like respite, security, peace.

My parents had been working tirelessly since they arrived in China from Indonesia as teenagers in 1966. They moved to China in hopes of a better education for themselves and their future family. The Cultural Revolution took place as soon as they arrived, so they found themselves without schooling and struggling for basic necessities like food. The only kind of work they were allowed to do was hard manual labor, so they walked from village to village, plowing farm after farm.

After several years of living in a harsh environment, far from what they dreamed of, they were given the opportunity to go to Hong Kong in 1972 with the help of a friend. After my father worked in many severe manual labor jobs, they decided to start their own import/export business while raising my elder sister, who is five years older than I. Their business grew and their family grew, which eventually afforded them the opportunity to purchase their first home—our first home—in their thirties. From the time I was born until I was six, my parents, my older sister, and I lived in a five-hundred-square-foot rental home in Hong Kong. I was happy there, but I didn't realize what was lacking in our living situation until my parents announced they had bought us a home. I watched my parents work hard each day of the year. They were never idle. They thought buying a home was a goal they could not possibly attain, but they did.

On December 16, 1984, we moved into a beautiful 1,180-square-foot (massive by Hong Kong standards) newly remodeled condominium overlooking the Victoria Harbour. My sister and I couldn't believe our luck. When we walked into our home, it felt like a mansion—fresh paint, gleaming hardwood floors, carpeted bedrooms, and wide views. Every room in the apartment was tailored to our needs: my sister and I picked out our own bedroom wallpaper and curtain fabric while our parents built us workstations for our homework; my father got an entertainment shelf for his stereo system, and my mother got a paradise kitchen with plenty of counter space.

After we moved in, we met some neighborhood kids. I would tag along with my older sister and her friends wherever they went, and that's when I met my childhood friend Susanna, who was also tagging along with her older brother. Since we are only eight months apart, we became as close as sisters and spent every spare minute together. In the summertime, Susanna and I would swim in the community pool three times a day, and she became a solid fixture in my home. Our home was often filled with friends and children; my mother would cook more than enough for every family to eat for five hours and still have food left over. My home was a happy one, and I loved it.

There is something powerful about the ownership of a home. It is connected to satisfaction and security, and even young children like myself can pick up on that. Even though I was only six at the time, I was proud of our home. I walked in that first day, and every day that followed, and thought, *This is ours.* Sometimes I wonder how I was so cognizant of the difference between renting and owning a home at such a young age; then I realize that I intuited this difference based on the transformations I saw in my parents when they became homeowners. I could feel how proud they were. They exhibited this satisfaction— and allowed us to participate in it—by having weekly cleanings every Sunday. Even if my sister and I tried to sleep in, my parents would wake us up and tell us to get started. Amid the vacuum whirring and the dishes clinking, I'd hear my parents calling, "Meeeiii, get up" (*mei* means "younger sister"). My mother would stretch the sheets tightly over each bed while my father shined the bronze furniture and cleaned our fish tank. Through the care they gave our home, they showed us the pride of homeownership. It was a profound lesson to learn at an early age, and it changed the course of my life.

While we lived in this home, we fell into a happy routine. On weekends, Susanna would come over, and we'd be tasked with grocery shopping for our families. We were happy to be together, though we were arguably a bit young to be so independent. We'd hold hands when we crossed street after street, laughing as we zipped through the crowds. We were about seven years old at the time, and though the market was chaotic and dirty, the vendors were especially kind and generous to us because of our age. We'd return home, our feet blackened by the filthy market streets, with proud smiles on our faces and food for our families.

During weekdays, while my parents worked from home, I'd get myself ready and walk to the bus stop before school. After school, I walked to my tutor's house to complete all my homework before heading home. I worked hard in school and was always one of the top three in my class. Because I excelled in elementary school, I was accepted to a reputable middle school that was a thirty-min-ute bus ride from home. My parents were always busy with their business; therefore, my sister and I were encouraged—or made—to be independent.

Despite the amount of time alone each day traveling to and from school and tutoring, I always looked forward to the evenings when my family would reconvene at home and have dinner together. *We were together, and we were happy.* My mom would cook delicious meals, and my father would begin his lecture of the day, which was our cue to roll our eyes and zone out to the familiar lull of our father's voice. If the story had ended here, it would be a happy one.

POWER OF HOME

In the years and decades that followed, my life became more fractured and chaotic, but I always found solace by closing my eyes and picturing my Hong Kong home, my family, my sister, and my best friend. I carried those memories with me to remind me of a time and a place when I felt happy and secure. My home sustained me mentally and emotionally for decades after leaving it. We often get so caught up in quantifiable measures of wealth and success that we forget about the value that lies in what cannot be seen. This is why homeownership is so important: your home doesn't stop meaning something to you when you leave it; it stays with you.

While I have gone on many adventures in my life, I often return to that memory of my early home. It has sustained me, encouraged me, sheltered me. In fact, every time I go back to Hong Kong, every time I pass that building, I always look up to the twenty-first floor window, unit 21E. *Home.*

I didn't feel the peace of homeownership again until I bought my adult home in San Jose decades later. When our family of four settled in (with one on the way), I felt that sense of security again. *I'm home.* Using the model that my parents demonstrated, I take pride in my home and find ways for my children to share in that. We make our beds each morning and share the cleaning chores. They see their parents take care of the home, maintain it, and improve it. We also eat dinner together each night, despite how hectic the day may have been.

I remind my children they will always remember this home. I hear them running through the halls, and I savor the sounds of laughter and family. *We are together, and we are happy.* My hope is that my children can continue to cement these feelings of security and contentment, and that when they lose their ways one day, which they will, they will always remember the peace of home. I hope that it will continue to comfort them, protect them, and surround them with the love of their family.

I've spent my professional career helping home buyers find this same sense of security and peace that I experienced in my Hong Kong home. There are two major reasons for purchasing a home, and they both have to do with security—owning a home is your first step toward *financial* security and building equity, and perhaps more importantly, it creates a sense of *emotional* security. It is a profound luxury to know you have a home to return to. It's a place of protection and fortification. It cannot be taken from you. It is yours.

Oftentimes when I'm working late at night in my home office, one of my children will wander in sleepy-eyed. For a moment, I am the child drifting into the room in Hong Kong, loaded with packaging materials and my parents hard at work. I am the child lulled by the sounds of my family in my home. Yet this time is different. I am the parent; this is my child. Just as my mother and father did for me, I hug my sleepy child and whisper, "Go back to bed." They return to the room they share with their siblings, and I return to my work, so that I can provide my family with more than walls and a roof. I can provide them with memories, security, and the pride of homeownership that will stay with them always. Just as my parents did for me, so I will do for my children.

ADVICE ON HOMEOWNERSHIP

Despite the obvious benefit of building equity, homeownership gives a family the power to improve its quality of life. This value is much harder to quantify but far exceeds a monetary one. Real estate transactions are often viewed as business deals when, in fact, real estate is a field that has ineffable impacts on one's life. These benefits aren't limited to the homeowner themselves; they extend to their children and grandchildren and can vastly alter a family's trajectory for generations.

CHAPTER TWO

SAD MEMORIES

When I was eleven years old and had happily lived in my family's Hong Kong condo for five years, my life began to crumble. In 1989, the summer before I started middle school, my best friend, Susanna, and her family moved to Canada. Without her, I was unmoored. My sister and I went to my parents and asked them if we could also move to Canada. We must have been fairly convincing because they listened to our proposal and took it seriously. In fact, they left my sister and I home alone for two weeks to explore Canada and even interviewed with the immigration department. While they were gone, a neighbor stopped by to check on us. When I answered the door, she asked, "What are you girls doing?" I answered plainly, "Ironing." She seemed suspicious until she looked behind me and saw the piles of clothes and linens. I guess the last thing she expected a child to be doing when home alone was ironing clothes! Little did she know, I was trying to prove my independence so that my family would relocate to Canada. When my parents returned, they explained that it wasn't feasible to relocate, as neither of them held higher education degrees. "We can't risk it financially," they explained. I tried to show a brave face, but I was devastated.

Not long after Susanna's move, I started at my new school, where I met a girl named Rebecca. We sat beside one another and sported matching ponytails and short bangs. We were both shy, but we each excelled in our own way. Rebecca was smart and helped me study; I was social and encouraged her to join me in extracurricular activities like volleyball, choir, and swimming. For the first time since Susanna moved, I found some happiness and purpose in school. At the same time, however, there was tension brewing at home. My parents' import/export suppliers had recently gone out of business, leaving my parents with no inventory to sell. As the financial stress mounted, so did their arguments.

During this time, they had also befriended a couple who quickly became fixtures in our lives. We started spending weekends together, and one of our favorite activities was hiking up to the Luck Changing Tower, a temple where your luck can reverse its course if you walk up the spiral staircase. We walked this tower almost every single weekend together for months. Then, one day, the couple didn't join us. My parents were evasive when we asked, but eventually they explained that they had loaned the couple much of their savings, which the wife had squandered. The family hid and never returned the money, and the wife ultimately ended up in jail for fraud.

Because of their mounting financial stress, our home became a tense environment. In hopes of finding a job, my dad decided to return to Indonesia, where all of his siblings lived. As a thirteen-year-old, I struggled to understand what was happening. All I knew was that within two years, Susanna had left, and now my father was leaving as well.

Once my dad left, my mother struggled to hold everything together for my sister and me. We talked to our dad rarely, as he worked on a small fishing boat in Indonesia and would come home every few months between his jobs. On his visits, he would show me pictures of the boats and regale me with stories of mosquito swarms and heavy rain swells. Even then, I understood that the work my father was doing was challenging manual labor again. He never complained about it, however. It was what he was willing to do for his family, and as always, I admired his efforts and ethics and vowed to be a heroic parent like him if given the chance.

After my father had been in Indonesia for several months, my mother informed us that his fishing business wasn't working out. He had been importing fish from Indonesia, but after all the fish died during one shipment, he was left with no product to sell. It was again another total loss. My father returned home, and soon they announced they had made a hard decision: "We have to sell the house." Time stopped. I could barely breathe. I remember begging my parents not to sell our home: "Please don't sell! It's our home! Why don't we just rent it out for now?" They said it was too hard to afford the mortgage payment and there was no other option. (Only recently my parents shared with me that the main reason they had to sell was because they took out a five-year mortgage rather than a thirty-year mortgage, so as not to saddle my sister and me with debt when we became adults. Their motive was noble, but it was not enough to spare us all from financial crisis.) If gaining a home was the greatest treasure of my childhood, then losing it had to be my greatest heartbreak.

LOST

I understood that we lost that home because of money—because my parents' business went under, because they made bad decisions about mortgages, because they loaned money to the wrong person. I remember thinking, *When you lose money, you lose things you love.* I understood that causal relationship: money could buy a home, security, family, and stability; losing it could rob you of all of those things just as quickly.

> **MONEY COULD BUY A HOME, SECURITY, FAMILY, AND STABILITY; LOSING IT COULD ROB YOU OF ALL OF THOSE THINGS JUST AS QUICKLY.**

After packing up our belongings, my parents found a small condo to rent. We went from a condo of 1,100 square feet down to one of 700 square feet. During this time, my father had returned home to Hong Kong and was working at a friend's watch factory. It was now my mother's turn to go to Indonesia and look for work. With my mother gone and my father working overtime most days, my sister and I had to do most of the housecleaning and cooking. My sister became my guardian, which I didn't enjoy. She and I were managing fine until our parents made a familiar announcement: "The rent is getting too expensive, and we're draining our bank account. We've got to move." My parents explained that rent can increase each year, oftentimes significantly. There was no guarantee that even if we could manage this year's rent, that we would be able to afford next year's rent. This time,

I didn't put up a fight. I saw how hard my parents were struggling, and since I'd already lost the home I loved, what was one more move?

My mother returned to help us with the move, and as always, she mopped and cleaned the apartment we were leaving. I asked her why she was cleaning a home that was no longer ours, and she explained that you always treat a home rented to you with respect so that if you ever need it again, the landlord will be happy to rent it back to you. (To this day, she even cleans hotel rooms out of respect before checking out.) We were becoming accustomed to packing and unpacking, so we did it one more time and moved into an even smaller place—five hundred square feet—with three bedrooms and one bath in an industrial area. We couldn't open the windows because of the smog, and needless to say, it was not a good experience.

I was still going to school with the same children, so they noticed we moved often. Most of the other kids had stable homes and rarely relocated. I longed for the stability and security of their lives. I remember feeling so ashamed of where I was living, so I tried to hide the fact that we resided across the harbor in the low-income industrial area. Since I was so much farther from school at this point, I left home at 6:20 a.m., walked to the subway station, took the subway across the harbor, walked to the bus stop, and then rode the bus to school. Day after day, I trudged through my life wishing I could go back home, but instead, I got off the subway at the industrial stop that felt nothing like the home I sought.

By this time, I was sixteen years old and in eleventh grade, preparing for the Hong Kong Certificate of Education Examination (HKCEE)—a test comprised of nine subjects taken over a four-month span. The exam would determine whether I could continue to advance my education into college preparatory grades, called twelfth and thirteenth grades in Hong Kong, and to which schools I might be accepted. It was an important step for my future, so after school, I would sit with a jug of lemon tea and study for hours, only stopping for quick "club sandwiches" made with bread, mayonnaise, peanut butter, jelly, and a sunny-side-up egg. By this time, my sister was in college, my mother was in Indonesia, and my dad worked a lot. I was growing accustomed to time spent alone, though I didn't enjoy it.

Just about a month before the series of exams started, my dad announced that he would be joining my mother in Indonesia to look for work. This was new. Previously one parent had always been in Hong Kong with my sister and me; now they were both leaving us. My mom came home to help my father move, and it was a painful time watching them pack up their things to leave us. Before they left, we put a camera on a timer and took a picture of our family in our tiny apartment. That was the last picture of the four of us together in our home country of Hong Kong.

My family's last photo in Hong Kong

YOU MUST BE EMPTIED BEFORE YOU CAN BE FILLED

When my mother first returned to Indonesia, she found a job at a hardware store. This was no Home Depot; it was a small, filthy, dusty store in a third-world country. My mother didn't know much about construction supplies, but she took her job seriously and always spoke of it with respect. I sometimes think about how hard it had to be for her to return to Indonesia. She and my father had left over two decades earlier as teenagers headed for the "big city" in China to advance their education. When they left, their families stayed behind. Their siblings must have looked up to my parents—young, resilient, hopeful, courageous. Over twenty years later, my mother, now in her late forties, returned with nothing. Her homecoming to Indonesia was more than a relocation; it was an admission that they had failed. Eventually, everyone encouraged my mother to utilize her passion for cooking and open a restaurant. In fact, my grandmother asked all my aunts and uncles to chip in money, silverware, pots and pans, and even tables and chairs to start this new business. Suddenly we were the ones in need of help.

Not long after the restaurant opened, my grandmother passed away. I saw how her death devastated my mother. She had been my mother's rock. I later realized I had the same supportive reliance on my own mother. When I call my mom with a problem, she listens. She typically says, "I can totally understand." That's all I need her to say. And she does understand. She's been knocked down over and over again, but she always gets back up. She understands despair, exhaustion, worry, and fear. She understands these feelings because she's lived her life *despite* them for decades.

My father also displayed the same survivor mentality upon his return to Indonesia. There was nothing he wouldn't do for his family. During each of our nightly family dinners in childhood, my father talked (and talked and talked) about being a good person. Being an ethical human was his highest goal, and he worked at that self-imposed ideal daily. At their Indonesian restaurant, my parents were constantly being harassed by neighborhood gangs who barged in, wielding knives, demanding money and food. Not only was my father unafraid, but he also embraced them and invited them to share a beer with him. His goal was not to please them; his goal was to touch their hearts so they felt loved. Many years later, in fact, one of the gangsters returned to the restaurant, stood in front of my father, and thanked him for inspiring to become an elected official in a nearby town. I often wondered why my father should have been pitied for his poor finances when he had the heart and soul of a hero. Likewise, could my mother really be considered poor when she had the riches of a loving, supportive mother? Should I note all of the things that were missing in my life when I had parents who consistently showed me the power of resilience and humility?

Watching my parents, I learned there are several ways to view hardships. So much of personal success depends not on what happened, but on how you view what happened. Though much of what was occurring in my family was confusing, the work ethic my parents modeled was uncompromising. My parents were never afraid to start at the bottom. There was no job they wouldn't do. Their focus was not on the manual labor or tedium of their jobs; it was on my sister and me. It

SO MUCH OF PERSONAL SUCCESS DEPENDS NOT ON WHAT HAPPENED, BUT ON HOW YOU VIEW WHAT HAPPENED.

would be easy to look back on my life and focus on myself and my troubles, but I knew my parents didn't do any of this to hurt us. In fact, it was the opposite. They did everything possible to ensure our successes, even if that meant they had to leave us behind. I admit, it was hard being the child in that scenario, but sometimes I think it must have been even harder being the parent. Our parents didn't abandon us; they fought for us at whatever costs.

My family certainly experienced hardships, and though they couldn't give us many things, they gave us the things that mattered— good examples. Oftentimes, as parents, we underestimate how our current behavior—from how we talk about work to how much we value our successes—sets the foundation for how the next generation will value their careers in the future. In my case, my parents modeled resilience, good character, a strong work ethic, and humility. They couldn't provide us with financial security, but in many ways they provided us with something more valuable: the tools to achieve financial successes ourselves, on our own terms, and in our own time. I have no excuses. I am not shocked by the unfairness of the world. I know that I will get knocked down, but because of my parents, I also know that I will always get back up.

To this day my mother can't look at that family picture we snapped on the last day in Hong Kong before they left us. She says it makes her heart ache. In many ways, the picture represents the life together that my family *could have* lived. But we didn't have the chance. Rather than sit with regret, however, I surround myself with hope. Where my mother and father see their failings, I see their successes. What they thought was a life of poverty was instead a life of riches, for they provided a solid foundation on which I have built a business, a family, a home.

ADVICE ON LOSS

Life is full of obstacles. With age, you realize that certain challenges are out of your control. It is impossible to disentangle the losses from the gains. You can't have one without the other. Yesterday's struggles give you power to embrace today's fortunes. Your success depends not on the obstacles themselves, but on how you view them. No matter how hard life seems now, know that better things lie ahead. You must be emptied before you can be filled.

CHAPTER THREE

FINANCIAL STRESS

After my parents left to return to Indonesia in search of work, our apartment was quiet and lonely. With my sister studying in college, I was usually home by myself. I would get up at three o'clock each morning and begin studying for the HKCEE exams before getting myself off to school. With the combination of my new freedom, family conflicts, chaotic moves, and growing sadness, my grades started slipping. I found it difficult to retain information, so I reread chapters over and over again. The exams were quickly approaching, and I had no time to waste. During this time, my mother returned to check on us, arriving in the middle of the night. When she peeked in on me sleeping, she gasped at how much weight I had lost in her absence. I awoke to her force-feeding me a protein shake with tears in her eyes.

Not long after my mother's short visit, she rejoined my father in Indonesia, and my sister and I were left home alone again. Shortly after, it was time for exams. I was anxious and stressed. The good news was that I ultimately scored high enough to earn a spot back at the same school. The bad news was that my sister was starting her third year of college—the internship year—and she decided to intern in Indonesia where my parents lived. I was speechless when she told me. What would become of me? She left in August before my twelfth-grade school year. So there I was: sixteen years old, living alone in a five-hundred-square-foot apartment in a rough industrial area of Hong Kong.

It was 1995, two years before the country's handover back to China. There was widespread anxiety about what life would look like in the coming years. Because of this, a lot of my classmates were being sent to schools in the United States, Canada, England, Australia, and other Western countries. My two best friends, Rebecca and Eliza, were among many close friends who moved away. I was left alone without my family or any of my close friends. I was sad and scared. Because of this, I hated airports for many years, as they reminded me of all the people I love who left me behind in my young life.

The start of school was still over a month away, and I was dreading it. Although I was fortunate to earn back a spot at my school, Marymount Secondary School, I didn't have any close friends left. Previously I had been active in school. Now, I was quiet, uninvolved, and lonely. When school started, it filled my days, but I was no longer involved in after-school activities, so I came home every evening to a silent, empty home. I would turn on the TV just to pretend like others were home with me. I cried myself to sleep every night. My parents couldn't phone often because of the price of international calls, though I often received calls from our angry landlord demanding rent. I felt lost and unprepared for the adult-sized world I found myself in.

About a month after I started school, my mom called, and I shared my struggles. She tried to comfort me by offering vague promises: "Oh, who knows? Maybe you can come to Indonesia and go to school here." That was all I needed to hear! The next day I excitedly went to school and told them I was leaving and to please give my hard-earned spot to someone else. Then, I went back home, called my mom, and said, "I told the school I'm leaving in a month!" My mom was shocked: "You quit school? Why did you do that? I wasn't serious about this!" I shrugged and told her I was coming to Indonesia regardless. I wanted to be with my family. Not long after our conversation, my dad returned to Hong Kong to help empty our tiny apartment. Soon, I began the journey back to my family. I wasn't sure what I would find in Indonesia, but I knew I would no longer be alone, and that was enough for me.

A FAMILY TORN APART

Once I got to Indonesia, it was clear that school was impossible. I could converse some in Indonesian, but I did not know how to read and write for the entrance test, and there was no international school option in the small town of Manado. So, at seventeen years old, instead of going to school, I helped at my parents' restaurant, strategizing how to sell enough plates of fried rice at fifty cents a plate to gross thirty dollars a day. I worked hard in the restaurant until midnight each night; on nights when we tested expanded hours, I worked until 5:00 a.m.

Just a month after my arrival, my sister and I both became ill. We lived among flies, cockroaches, rats, and lots of mosquitoes. In fact, one of the biggest risks living in Indonesia was contracting malaria. Though doctors ruled that out, our fevers persisted for three weeks. My parents gathered our aunts and pastor and propped us up in bed to pray over us. Remarkably, I woke the next day feeling better, but my sister didn't. She ended up in the hospital diagnosed with dengue fever. She was extremely ill, and the doctor said she could have easily died had she been younger and weaker. Luckily, after days in the hospital, she got her strength back and ultimately made a full recovery.

After my sister regained her strength, we started to make friends. We were popular in the small town since most of the Manadonese people had only seen Hong Kongese in movies. We had many cousins and other relatives nearby, which was a new experience for us. The only entertainment in town was the Matahari Mall, which consisted of a supermarket, department stores, and an arcade. There was also a movie theater, but since it wasn't safe to take a microbus there, we rarely went. We got excited when rarely seen tourists showed up in town and we could practice our basic English with them. We slowly developed friendships with some tourists, but we were only allowed to socialize with them in the restaurant, since being friendly with Caucasian men was considered inappropriate and would incite small-town gossip.

Though I had gotten ill, was unschooled, and worked tire-lessly each day, I reveled in my good fortune: I was with my family, and I was happy, despite our (even) poorer living conditions. The new chaos of cousins all around me was a welcome antidote to my periods of isolation and loneliness. Being reunited with my family was extremely healing, but it also put me in contact with my parents' struggles once again. Years of financial stress continued to erode their marriage.

One night after the restaurant closed, my parents called a family meeting. I felt uneasy, as I had noticed their arguments escalating in recent days. We assembled around the dining table, and my mom gently stated, "Your father and I are splitting up. Your father will be leaving." Hearing this after finally being reunited with my family was devastating. I looked at my sister and hoped she could say something to save their marriage, but she had been here even longer than me, and she probably had sensed it coming. Besides, as the older sibling, she was much more mature to handle the news. I tried to reason with them, but my father remained unmoved. In a desperate attempt to get through to him, to let him know how much I was hurting, I yelled in his face. My father was a traditional man, with a large, stoic presence. He demanded respect, and we knew it. We never talked back to him, let alone yelled at him, but the anger and sadness I felt rushing through me made me frantic to keep us together. Before I knew it, I slapped him in the face. *I slapped my father!* My mom rushed over to hold me, while my father furiously raised his hand in retaliation. He paused, however, and stopped himself.

Moments later, I knelt before him and begged for forgiveness. He refused to talk to me, and my mom pushed us out of the room. "Everything is going to be fine," she reassured us. "Go to sleep." I crawled into the bed I shared with my sister and broke down. I did not sleep all night. I replayed slapping my father over and over again. I had worked so hard to find my way back to my family, and now it was over. No family to reunite with. No home to find my way back to.

I waited until the sun came up, and I heard my mom readying the restaurant. I went to her with swollen eyes and an aching heart. She tried to comfort me: "Don't think about it anymore. Go back in, and try to sleep. Don't worry about helping in the restaurant today." But how could I follow her advice? My entire world was crumbling.

Though I felt like a heartbroken child on the inside, I was aware and mature enough to see exactly what had happened in their marriage. Their split was a by-product of being so stressed financially. It made sense. They were out of energy; we were all out of energy. I understood that it would be easier to let the family divide at that point, but I couldn't let that happen. I had come too far to let our home life crumble in this way—and all because of money.

FOR BETTER OR FOR WORSE

Even after another two decades of continued arguments, my parents did not end up separating; in fact, they are still married today. Seeing them together today, it's hard to imagine their decades of marital struggles. They still do not see eye to eye on many issues, but they have learned to keep any occasional hostility toward each other under control, just like any married couple. Their brush with divorce, however, imprinted on me—I understood that even the most solid of marriages aren't immune to the pressures of financial hardships. Financial stress can be the catalyst for losing everything, not just houses and cars, but families and trust. I know that financial strain makes even the strongest family unstable. It creates cracks that oftentimes cannot be fixed.

FINANCIAL STRESS CAN BE THE CATALYST FOR LOSING EVERYTHING, NOT JUST HOUSES AND CARS, BUT FAMILIES AND TRUST.

During financial hardships, you feel out of control. You feel like a force is set in motion, and no matter how hard you try to slow it down or stop it, you can't fight the momentum. This feeling of powerlessness haunted me for decades. I remember thinking that I would work hard, as my parents had done, and find some way to take control of my own financial security in the future. I didn't want to feel that my life was rolling away from me ever again.

One of the goals of writing this book is to share my struggles and offer hope to those of you in the middle of hardships. As you will discover in later chapters, I offer strategies to avoid the obstacles my own family encountered. I want my story to help you avoid financial crises and take control of your financial security. Most importantly, however, I want to help you keep your home, your family, your sanity. These are the treasures in life, and with the right mindset and planning, you can hold tightly to the things you value most.

ADVICE ON TAKING CONTROL OF YOUR FINANCES

Life has ups and downs, and you absolutely must prepare for them. I do not want to be financially *reactive*; I want to be financially *proactive*. For this reason, I'm constantly thinking about the worst-case scenario and how I can prevent it. For some people, this might seem like fear-based thinking, but when you've lived through it once, it changes your perspective.

My parents did several things wrong, including lending money to someone who wasn't trustworthy and working with a short mortgage loan. Another mistake they made was relying on one source of income. When their import/export business failed, there was no other income.

I hope I can get people to think proactively about their future financial security. As we will discuss fully in later chapters, this is why I tell clients who are able, to buy one home to live in and one more as an investment property. If my parents had done this when we were in our Hong Kong condo, then when their business went under, we could have lived off the rental property's passive income. Of course it would have been a tight budget, but we wouldn't have lost our only home and gotten into a tailspin that took us decades to fully recover from.

CHAPTER FOUR

A LIFE-CHANGING MINDSET

Adapting to life in a third-world country was not easy. I found solace in the American movies that played on the restaurant television. I soon realized that hearing the English language spoken while reading the Indonesian subtitles could improve my proficiency in both. Despite how poor we were, the living expenses were extremely low. My parents assured me that I could continue to work in the restaurant and eventually marry a good, wealthy man in town.

That sounded like a good life for a typical girl in the Asian culture. But I kept thinking, *This can't be my life forever.* I grew tired of well-meaning family and friends telling me about the eligible bachelors they knew. It was hard to persuade them that I wasn't thinking of marriage at this age. After all, I was only seventeen. What I really wanted to think about was going to school—somewhere far away from here. Out of curiosity, and knowing my best friends were being sent to the United States, I wrote to several American universities requesting information. I would then carefully study the brochures they sent, comparing costs for boarding, books, and tuition. I was trying to shoot for the stars, aiming for goals that I didn't believe could happen. I decided I would much rather dream about it, fantasize about a new life, and see how far I could go. I remember staring at one particular brochure image of a female student studying on a grassy, tree-lined quad amid beautiful brick university buildings. *I want to be her.* I started speaking to her in my broken English. I would tell her how beautiful her school was and how I wished I could join her there.

I continued to write to my friend Rebecca, who had moved to Los Angeles right before I moved to Indonesia. She told me about her new life in the United States. It sounded fun and carefree. I wrote back telling her about my struggles in Indonesia. I told her this was not the life I wanted to be in forever. In her response, she included an application to Santa Monica College and a note that said, "Why don't you attend my school? I will try to help." Her plan sounded promising.

My parents didn't know I had been doing college research, much less submitted an application to Santa Monica College. A few weeks later, I received an I-20—an approval from the school to accept me as a foreign student. This was required paperwork to apply for a student visa at the US Embassy. I was thrilled just holding the paper. I shared this exciting news with my parents, and their response was practical and unsurprising—"You know we don't have money, right? LA is a big city, and it's too expensive! If you want to go back to school, why don't you return to Hong Kong?" Going to LA sounded too unrealistic to them; after all, they had never been there, and neither had I. We only knew what we saw in the movies. LA meant Hollywood, beaches, seagulls, sunsets, and shiny people.

What my parents didn't realize at the time was that they were huge inspirations for me educationally. Both of them had barely finished high school because China was going through a revolution at the time, so they never had a technical background or one specific profession. What they did have was survival skills. They started with nothing and went from Indonesia to China to Hong Kong. They had always taught me through their actions to grab an opportunity and go with it. That's what I was trying to do now. I felt like I was walking in the same shoes as them—I was starting with nothing and going from Hong Kong to Indonesia to America. I knew I could do it because I'd watched them do it. Sure, I watched them struggle, but I also saw them be resilient, resourceful, and persistent. I knew I had those qualities in me as well. Because of their examples, I had a realistic expectation of the effort I would have to put in to make this transition work. Like my parents, I wouldn't focus on the hard work and sacrifice; I would instead focus on the security it could eventually afford me.

When I announced my intentions to go to America, my parents offered me two options—go back to Hong Kong and repeat the grade I'd skipped (which would require me to be with a younger class of students who used to look up to me) or stay in Indonesia and run the restaurant together. "This can be yours," they offered. They made a good case for me to stay, pointing out that I could make money in Indonesia and go on vacations to California instead. Already interested in how far money could stretch in other countries, I countered, "But when you go to the United States for vacation, your money is worth so little. I would much rather work there, make decent money, and come back for a luxury vacation in Indonesia."

My sister had already moved back to Hong Kong a month prior to finish up her last year of college. I told my parents I was also moving back to Hong Kong and would apply for a US student visa. My parents asked how I would show the embassy that I could afford to study abroad. I wasn't sure, but I thought I'd figure it out.

When I left Indonesia to join my sister in Hong Kong, I knew my parents were in pain. My mom broke down at the airport. My dad did not smile. Now I understand that he was probably upset that he could not do anything to stop me. My parents were together, but their relationship was still rocky. It had felt for a while that our family was unlucky. I hated being so selfish by leaving, but staying in the middle of their situation didn't feel like an option. I knew they needed to figure their relationship out for themselves, just as I needed to figure my life out for myself. I cried saying goodbye. Another airport, another loss.

My family at the Indonesia airport sending me off to Hong Kong

Once I was in Hong Kong, I stayed at a friend's house. My sister was staying with another friend while she finished her last year of school. During this time, she and I started meeting for dinner often. It was nice to cultivate the relationship we had ignored for so long. But my focus was still on my plan to study in America. It was 1996, and the handover of Hong Kong back to China was only a year away. Most of my friends were convinced that it was impossible to get my student visa application approved because my family had no money.

Rather than let their comments deter me, however, I put all of my efforts into collecting all of the documents I could think of to present a strong case for visa approval—my academic reports, extra-curricular activities certificates, teachers' references, high school testi-monials, family pictures, my aunt's financial statements with simple translations, even my piano recital certificate and my parents' Indo-nesian bank statements. Once I organized and categorized a folder, I felt like I was ready to try for a student visa. This could be my ticket to a new life.

FIRST IMPRESSIONS MATTER

My parents always taught me that first impressions were important. It was summer, and I wore my favorite light-blue turtleneck sweater, skirt, and my five-year-old Doc Martens boots. I hoped my outfit could convince the interviewer that I belonged to a wealthy family. I went to the embassy three hours before it opened to avoid the perpet-ually long lines. I was the first person there, and I sat on a bench and waited until they opened. Once inside, I had to turn in my folder and wait to be called. I was so nervous because this was *it*—this was the moment that would decide what my future was going to look like. Most of the other applicants had family members and friends with them, but I sat alone. I kept hearing the embassy workers call names, but never mine. *Why aren't they calling me? What did I do wrong?* Finally they called my name.

I walked up to the window, and the embassy interviewer said in English, "Good job, you're the first one to have a complete package." That was why my name wasn't called! He asked me why I wanted to go to the United States. He asked about my background. I told him I had gone to Indonesia for ten months to help out my parents at the restaurant. I showed him a picture of my extended family in Indonesia. I showed him my aunt's land deed and bank statements. The bank statement was in Indonesian rupiah currency, and at that time, one US dollar equaled three thousand rupiah. It looked like a lot of money for someone who was not familiar with the conversion rate. Hopefully, that would work in my favor. He was very impressed by everything I had presented to him. Then he asked me to show off some Indonesian. I was nervous. I obliged, but remember the words being all wrong and making no sense. Luckily, he didn't know the difference. "That sounds really cool," he said. Then he continued, "I'm going to give you an approval." I was frozen. He repeated, "You're approved. Go next door to pay the fee." I broke down in tears: "Oh thank you, thank you, thank you, thank you!"

At this point, my entire body was shaking. I gathered all of my documents, paid my fee, and ran out of the embassy to find the nearest pay phone. I dialed my parents in Indonesia with the few dollars I had, saying, "I got it, I got it. I got approved, and I'm going to the United States!" To be honest, I don't remember what my parents' responses were, but my dad recently reminded me of what he had said. He was shocked, but he knew neither he nor my mom could have stopped me. So he said, "I am so proud of you to have accomplished this, but we've never been to the United States, so there is no advice that we can give you. You're on your own now. Go ahead and explore. If all fails, it's OK to come back; we will still be proud of you."

After we hung up, I went straight into planning mode. Both my friend Rebecca and my cousin David had attended school in the United States the year before and had returned to Hong Kong for summer vacation. They were attending Santa Monica College, and it made sense that I should tag along with my cousin since he was my only family there. We made our flight and transportation plans, and I wrote a letter to my parents stating how much money I would need and when I would be leaving. I itemized the costs of my travel, books, tuition, and insurance. I had researched how much rent would cost. I asked them to help in any way they could and told them I would get a job and figure out other expenses when I got there.

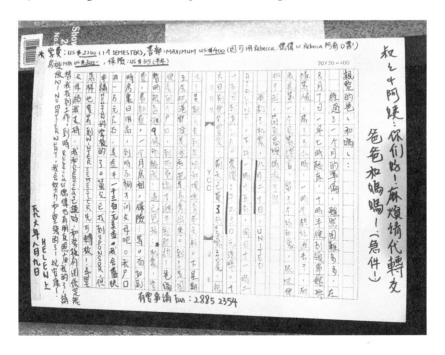

The letter I sent my parents prior to leaving for the US

I scheduled my flight to leave Hong Kong on August 22, 1996. I spent several days packing everything I could think of I knew I could get in the United States, although for a much higher price. So I packed up an alarm clock, hygiene products, and comforters that were given to me by my aunt. I wanted to save every penny I could. I had a farewell dinner with my friends before I left and called my parents.

On the morning of my departure, I was anxious and excited. I put on the same blue sweater I'd worn to the embassy, hoping it would continue to bring me good luck. At the airport, I checked my bags and waited at the gate with my sister. Suddenly, I felt light-headed, my heart started racing, and I realized what this meant: I didn't know when I would come back home again. I wouldn't be able to ask my parents to come save me if things didn't work out. I would have to figure everything out on my own. I looked at my sister and said, "I'm scared. What am I doing?" She answered with teary eyes, "You're leaving." I trembled and hugged her. It was a long and difficult goodbye; we would be going our separate ways from this point on. Still, I made my choice, and I followed my cousin onto the plane. I had just turned eighteen years old, and *that* was the path that changed my life.

> **I WOULDN'T BE ABLE TO ASK MY PARENTS TO COME SAVE ME IF THINGS DIDN'T WORK OUT. I WOULD HAVE TO FIGURE EVERYTHING OUT ON MY OWN.**

My sister and I at the Hong Kong airport before my first flight to the United States, wearing my lucky blue sweater

DIFFICULTIES AHEAD

It was a long flight, and I cried the entire time. When we landed, my cousin and I exited the plane to the tarmac. It was the first time I'd been in the United States and the first time my skin felt the California air. It was amazing—warm, but not sticky, with a cool breeze and deep-blue skies. I fell in love instantly. I tagged along with my cousin to the van that picked us up. The driver was Chinese, which made me feel at ease, but when he said it would be $90 per person, I was shocked. Before I left, I had withdrawn my entire savings from all the years of collecting red envelopes during Chinese New Year, which totaled about US$1,000. I was hoping this would last me awhile and hadn't factored losing almost 10 percent of my net worth in one car ride on my first day in America.

We stayed at my cousin's friend's apartment for the first several days. I needed to call my parents but was unsure how to use the phone. I called the operator, who agreed to connect me. I knew it would be expensive, so I only spoke with them for a few minutes. I said, "I'm here. I'm safe. Don't worry about me. I'll figure things out." When I hung up, I cried. Little did I know, that short call cost $50. I hugged the stuffed animal I had packed in hopes of feeling less alone. I set a timer on the camera and took our picture—a girl and her stuffed Doraemon in America.

My stuffed animal and I on one of our first nights in America

A few days later, I moved into my new apartment, sharing a room with my cousin's girlfriend. I cried hysterically every night because I missed home so much. The apartment was about ten blocks from Santa Monica College. I tagged along with my cousin and his girlfriend to meet their friends for lunch. Having already spent 15 percent of my net worth on an airport shuttle and a call home, I couldn't justify spending money at a restaurant, so I didn't order food. "Are you going to eat?" my cousin asked. I casually responded, "No, I'm not hungry." But I was hungry; I was starving.

By this time, school was starting in a week or so, and I had to find a permanent place to live. I didn't like going out on my own yet because everything was foreign and intimidating. I did not even know how to cross a street because the traffic lights looked so different compared to Hong Kong. *What does that blinking hand mean?* I walked over ten huge blocks and went to the International Students Center of Santa Monica College, and I looked for people seeking a roommate on a bulletin board. I copied all the phone numbers down, went to a pay phone, and called each one. Finally I spoke with a girl with an accent who agreed to meet. Her name was Kim, and she was from Korea. Together we found a one-bedroom furnished apartment a few blocks from school. It cost $650 a month, which we agreed to split, with one of us taking the bedroom and the other taking the living room.

THE ART OF ADAPTING

Once Rebecca came back to the United States, I begged her to spend the night with me, and she did. It felt wonderful to have a close friend and a piece of home with me. The next day, she showed me how to navigate the bus system. I realized the mass transit system, unlike that of Hong Kong, was outdated and extremely inconvenient. She referred me to a part-time job with an amazing family restaurant in Beverly Hills. I thought to myself, *Is this the 90210 I used to watch on TV?* I was ecstatic, despite the fact that it would take me over an hour on two or three different bus lines in order to get to work. I didn't mind because I had to survive.

I quickly realized that most international students came from money, as evidenced by their luxury cars and active social lives. When I declined to join their parties because of work, one boy laughed and asked, "Work? Why would you need to do *that*? Aren't you a foreign student? All foreign students are rich; that's how we can afford to come here." He said his parents gave him $2,000 a month for allowances. I almost threw up. I was trying to keep my monthly expenses under $200 a month before rent, and I only made $360 a month! It was surreal being so poor surrounded by so much wealth.

I tried to fit into the Indonesian crowd, but since they were so wealthy, I couldn't fit in. Even though I had been born and raised in Hong Kong, I couldn't fit into the Hong Kong group, as I didn't feel right to be speaking Cantonese while being in the United States. I felt that I needed to adapt to the society. However, my English was still rudimentary, so I didn't fit in with Americans either. American students were outspoken—too outspoken. They frequently raised their hands and interjected comments in class. In Hong Kong, we are taught to listen; we do not speak up until we are asked to do so. These differences left me feeling lost and unmoored. This was made worse when an older American on the street asked me, "Are you Chinese?" I snapped, "No! I am from Hong Kong." He looked puzzled and asked, "Isn't that the same thing?" Hong Kong was still months away from July 1, 1997—the handover back to China. Most Hong Kong residents were proud of the association with Britain and dreaded being identified as Chinese, whom they thought to be less educated, less progressive, and much less advanced than Hong Kong. I was raised with such prejudice, and how wrong was I? The conversation with this man only highlighted how lost I felt. *Who am I? Where do I belong?*

Very soon, I found myself drawn to diverse groups of kids from different countries. Most were from Asia, though some had come to the United States at a much younger age. Most of us spoke English with different levels of accent, but I was happy because we spoke

English with each other. I finally felt at ease; I could fit into the Asian culture while I was speaking this country's language: English.

Rebecca and I met up daily, and she would drive me to the market to shop. We strategized how to stay fed using as little money as possible. We agreed that we could just bring a bottle of water and two slices of multigrain bread for lunches, which should fill our stomachs. We bought instant noodles that cost only twenty cents each. My roommate had a rice cooker, and if I were ever so lucky as to be allowed to use it, I would make myself a sunny-side up over rice and sprinkle some soy sauce—yum! In just two weeks, I had secured an apartment and a job at an American diner for five dollars an hour on Saturdays and Sundays. The most daunting part of the job was learning the names of different bakery items, which I had never even seen before—croissants, pecan rolls, schnecken, scones, bran muffins, zucchini muffins, little crescents, oatmeal cookies, and more. I had so much to learn.

I was the youngest employee, but the owners noticed I worked hard. Soon, they gave me a twenty-five cent raise. My English wasn't good enough to wait tables, but one day they asked me to take lunch orders over the phone. *Uh-oh*, I thought. I wrote my orders phonetically. One customer asked for a burrito. "Boo-ree-toe," I echoed back. They asked for guacamole. "OK, gwa-ca-mo-lee."

Working at this restaurant reminded me of my parents' restaurant, so I treated it as if it was my family's business: I knew the importance of taking care of the customers. My bosses were happy with my work ethic and continued to give me a quarter raise every few weeks. They even entrusted me to balance their cash

I TREATED IT AS IF IT WAS MY FAMILY'S BUSINESS: I KNEW THE IMPORTANCE OF TAKING CARE OF THE CUSTOMERS.

register. I used the skills I had learned while working at my parents' restaurant and counted the cash like a banker and ran the calculator with my speedy fingers to balance all checks. I worked fast and always greeted customers with a smile. One day as we were about to close the restaurant, a man came in asking to place a large takeout order. Even though we could have said no, I decided to help him. After I stayed late to get the order together, the man tipped me ten dollars! I was ecstatic and felt rich.

A year later, I was promoted to waitress, which was the highest compensated position because I could now earn my own tips. It was time to test my English (and my understanding of American cuisine): "How would you like the eggs? Over easy, over medium, over hard, scrambled, sunny-side up, hard broiled, or poached? Would you like bacon, sausage, or ham? Would you like hash browns, french fries, or home fried potatoes? Would you like white, whole wheat, rye, sourdough bread or plain, sesame seed, onion, or everything bagel? If not, how about an English muffin?" It was a never-ending question for just one dish!

I woke at five o'clock on the weekend mornings to make it to the bus stop on time. While I waited at the connecting bus stop at the busy intersection of Santa Monica and Sepulveda Boulevards, I would watch the shiny cars speeding past. I often felt angry and embarrassed for all I lived without. I'd look at each polished, relaxed driver passing me and think, *I'm going to drive a nicer car than* you *one day. And I'm going to drive a nicer car than* you *one day. And I'm going to drive a nicer car than* you *one day.* When I got off work, I would walk forty-five minutes to the other side of Beverly Hills for the Blue Bus line rather than the VTA line so I could save $0.75 in bus fare.

I spent weekends working at the diner and weekdays studying at school. I did well academically and enjoyed the small classes. I learned to speak up more and built good relationships with the teachers. I finally felt like I had become that girl on the cover of the college brochure I received. Whereas California residents pay $12 a semester unit for community college, foreign students pay $130 a semester unit. Paying more than ten times other students motivated me to finish the junior college program as quickly as possible. I finished in one and a half years, and then I had to figure out my next step.

During that first year, Rebecca had introduced me to several friends, so my social life eventually began to blossom.

Just like any teenager, a boy started offering me rides home and to work. I accepted and quickly became accustomed to the convenience of a car. We spent more time together and began dating. What was harder to get used to, however, was his temper. He would get mad about small things and wanted to know where I was at all times. I was not allowed to speak with other boys. Because of this, my social life diminished again, and Rebecca was the only one I could keep as a friend. Still, I put up with the jealousy because it was convenient not to walk or wait for buses. I thought our relationship was "normal" and that all couples fought.

Meanwhile, since I finished all of the prerequisite courses by February 1998, I had until August to start school. However, I had to wait for a couple of more months before I'd know which university would accept me. So I added a second job at a Hong Kong–style restaurant and worked seven days a week in hopes of saving up enough money to see my parents. I was offered only $3 an hour there and had to split my tips with the owner, but I didn't care because it was money earned, and I got to work with Rebecca. We had so much fun working together, and she'd drive me home at the end of the day. On days we didn't work together, I walked over an hour to go home to save the cost of bus fare.

My plan was to leave the United States in April and return by August to start my junior year in a university. I would stay in Indonesia for two months and then in Hong Kong for two months. I asked my sister to help me pay for a flight from Singapore to Indonesia so I could surprise my parents. I canceled my lease, as I could not afford to pay it while I was gone. I put away my belongings in my boyfriend's apartment, and I eventually found a reasonable flight for $545 that would fly me to Singapore, then Hong Kong, and then back to the United States. I wanted to say I was excited to return to Asia, but I didn't have a home anymore. I was, however, very excited to see my parents finally.

ADVICE ON BEING FAR FROM HOME

Though it was challenging being far away from my home country and my family, I learned many valuable lessons that continue to inform my decisions today. Firstly, I learned that whether you are in a small restaurant in Indonesia or a bustling diner in LA, the best way to advance your job status is to provide a pleasant experience for your customers. This lesson informs every interaction that I have with my HAYLEN Real Estate clients. A kind word and a smile can make even the most rigid of customers/clients relax and connect with you and your service in a more compassionate way.

Secondly, no matter where you are or who you are with, it's important that you find your own identity. You may not fit into a particular group, but if you know your own place and your own value, you will not feel excluded. This was a hard lesson to learn, and one that I sometimes feel I am still learning, but having a strong identity at a young age propels you personally and professionally for the rest of your life.

Lastly, don't be a barrier to your own success. When you have self-limiting beliefs, you impede your own path to success. For example, even when I couldn't afford to buy myself a comb, I never focused on what I lacked; instead, I viewed it as an opportunity to remind myself that I was resourceful and would find ways to afford what I needed and wanted. Focus on your own skills and talents to forge a path toward the life that you seek.

CHAPTER FIVE

FACING RACISM IN ASIA

I t took twenty-four hours to make it to the small town of Manado, where my parents lived. Because I wanted to surprise my parents, I arranged for a family friend to drive me to their restaurant. I was at that point almost twenty years old, and I walked into the restaurant in a skirt and high heels. My parents turned to see, but the sun was blinding their eyes, and they didn't recognize me, as I did not dress like my old self anymore. When I walked much closer, my mother looked at me; she screamed and gathered me in her arms. My dad followed, and we held each other tightly and cried uncontrollably. It was a lovely welcome and reminded me that anywhere my parents were, this is home. The smell of my mother's hair, the grip of my father's hand—it all felt so familiar. I felt safe, loved, and happy.

Manado is such a small town that my mother had to travel to the capital of Indonesia, Jakarta, in order to purchase simple equipment for the restaurant. I offered to travel with her to Jakarta for a few days. Jakarta is very different from Manado, a much bigger city with a lot more entertainment. I loved being in a big city again with my mother and stayed with my cousin Hengki, whose house was located in a gated Chinese community. We were only supposed to be there for three days, but I had so much fun that I begged my mom to postpone our return trip again and again, and *again*.

RIOTS ERUPT

On May 12, 1998, we picked up Hengki's little sister, Nancy, from her college dorm and went to a mall to visit another cousin, Heidi. As we were leaving the mall, people started running past us toward the exit. We overheard people yelling about a protest at Nancy's university. We hurriedly ran to our car and got onto the road. Jakarta is known for its heavy traffic, but this gridlock was something entirely different. We saw chaos on the road, and it took us three hours to finally get back safely to my cousin's house.

As soon as we got back, neighbors informed us the protest had been started by university students over the Asian financial crises that had caused mass unemployment and food shortages. It quickly transformed into a riot blaming Chinese and non-Muslim people because they were considered the wealthier demographic. Many Chinese people had moved to Indonesia and other Southeast Asian countries for decades to escape Communism and instability in China. Since then, Chinese immigrants had worked extremely hard to build their wealth by building businesses wherever they landed. As time passed, Chinese became the wealthier ethnic group, and they would employ the local Indonesians to be their workers. For many years, the Indonesian government restricted the Chinese culture by eliminating Chinese surnames and Chinese business names, and it even prohibited any Chinese languages to be spoken or taught.

This conflict erupted before our eyes that day in Jakarta. Indonesian rioters profiled people with smaller eyes and lighter skin tone. The media warned that no one should leave home, but our teenage neighbor didn't listen. He put on his helmet and biked away. Hours later, he returned with a bloody face because the rioters had ripped off his helmet to check his eyes before beating him badly. He was lucky, as he made it back alive, unlike many others. We turned on the TV and learned the downtown district was hit the hardest. Rioters stormed Chinese shops, and owners' homes were often above their businesses. Rioters gang-raped grandmothers, mothers, and daughters, and then torched them in front of their fathers, brothers, and sons. We turned on the radio and heard the excruciating cries of people calling in for help: "Please help us, they're coming, they're coming!"

My mom was the only adult in the house, and she tried to distract my cousins and me from listening to the horrific news on TV and radio. Since our gated community was mainly Chinese, we became a target also. All the men, including Hengki, were tasked to guard the community twenty-four hours a day with any kind of weapons they could find at home—axes, plows, knives, shovels, and so forth. Following my mother's example, I tried to remain calm. I heard about fires being set in Chinese-occupied homes, so I found a ladder that I propped up so we could climb to the roof in case we needed to escape. I didn't know what we would do once we got to the roof, but it seemed better than not doing anything. Three times, we heard people yelling to be ready, as the rioters were coming in, but somehow the guards were able to fend them off.

On the second night, we walked toward a restaurant within the community, as we hadn't prepared enough food at home. The skyline

THE SKYLINE WAS ENGULFED IN SMOKE. IT LOOKED LIKE A WAR ZONE FROM A MOVIE.

was engulfed in smoke. It looked like a war zone from a movie. We lived in fear for two days, while my mom, hidden in the bedroom, desperately sought a way out of town. We talked about driving to the airport, but we'd heard that the highways to the airport had been shut down. The streets were still filled with rioters looking for targets to kill and rape. The telephone line worked intermittently, and my dad was also working tirelessly from Manado to find a way to get us out.

On the third day of the riots, through my dad's connection, my mom told us that someone would pick us up the next morning to take us to the airport. She explained that we were not to wear any makeup or jewelry; we could only wear old, dark T-shirts, jeans, and running shoes. If we wore anything that brought attention to ourselves, we could be in danger. The next morning, we woke around 5:00 a.m. and proceeded to dress as plainly as possible. Then, we waited for a knock on the door. Finally we heard it and opened the door to an Indonesian man who had been instructed by a family friend to drive my cousin's car and drive us to the airport. He was our best shot, so even though he was Indonesian, we trusted that he would protect us from the rioters. The highway was still closed, so the driver explained that we would be taking smaller roads through villages to get to the airport. This was an extremely dangerous plan because the villages were filled with Indonesians, but it was our only option.

He gave us stern instructions that since he was not Chinese, he was the only person who would roll down his window if we were stopped. Hengki sat in the front passenger seat because he had darker skin and bigger eyes and could pass for an Indonesian. My mom, Nancy, and I sat in the back seat. We were shaking with fear. We ducked in the car as much as possible. As we were driving slowly through one village, we were stopped. The driver accidentally rolled down my mom's window instead of his own. I panicked and lunged over to quickly roll the window back up. I had no idea what dangers were out there.

ESCAPE

I don't remember how long it took to get to the airport. It seemed like hours. When we arrived, we cried. My mom bought plane tickets for all of us, and we finally felt safe. Only seventeen people made it to the plane that day to return to Manado. We looked at each other and knew how extremely lucky we were. As we made our layover stop, we saw many people from different parts of Indonesia on their way to Manado to escape the riots throughout the country. Manado is a Christian town, and local Manadonese had smaller eyes and a lighter skin tone, so many people fled there for safety. Many more escaped to nearby countries like Singapore and Australia, while others fled to the United States and England. There were never accurate statistics on the riot's violence, but we know over one thousand people died, and hundreds of women were raped, tortured, and burned to death within three days.

I blocked out these experiences for many years. It wasn't until I had children that I would sometimes have a stray memory hit me, usually at night, and leave me shaking. I remember one time walking to my husband in the living room, trembling, and asking him to hold me tight so I could convince myself I was safe. I can't even imagine how scared my mom must have been to be responsible for three kids in this situation. Likewise, I can't fathom how frustrated and helpless my dad must have felt not to be able to reach us or help us.

I will tell my children the story of the riots one day, but for today, I'm just grateful to have them tucked into their warm beds in a safe place where I can protect them. When I panic that they might one day feel the same fear I felt in the days of the riots, I remind myself that situations like these do make a person stronger.

As I write this, the United States is experiencing both the coronavirus pandemic and our own civil unrest due to racial discrimination, particularly toward black individuals. Riots broke out throughout major cities across the country, and protests were being held globally. Our world is tired of racism, but more importantly, we are tired of the leadership that has created a culture of division and blame. We should remember that the current pandemic and racism is not just a US problem but a global problem that has existed for many years. We need to remind ourselves that we can each be a part of the solution through our own efforts and our professions. Leaders are often the cornerstones who set the culture of their organizations. Our society is suffering from a culture of division, as people use every opportunity to divide us by calling out race, culture, beliefs, political opinions, wealth, and the list goes on and on.

Having become a leader in organized commercial real estate, I am extremely proud to have helped break the stereotypical profile of the commercial real estate industry; now, instead of the stereotype, we see a

> WE NEED TO REMIND OURSELVES THAT WE CAN EACH BE A PART OF THE SOLUTION THROUGH OUR OWN EFFORTS AND OUR PROFESSIONS. LEADERS ARE OFTEN THE CORNERSTONES WHO SET THE CULTURE OF THEIR ORGANIZATIONS.

diverse mix of genders, colors, ages, and religions within our membership and leadership—all working toward a common goal: elevating the commercial real estate industry standard through education.

We should take pride in what we, as individuals, have accomplished, and what we stand for. I hope that you will join me in turning the tide against cultural division one organization at a time and lead the way for others to follow. We may only create a ripple, but the example we set can build to a wake, and hopefully, someday, a wave.

Martin Luther King once said, "Darkness cannot drive out darkness; only light can do that. Hate cannot drive out hate; only love can do that." I pray that our society will stop the divisions of people; instead, we will lead the way and work toward a common goal for the greater good of all humans.

ADVICE ON DISCRIMINATION

For those who did not survive these horrific events, I can only pray that we, as modern human beings, can learn from them. There is a tremendous amount of discrimination, even among people of the same race. Over twenty years after Hong Kong was returned back to China, many Hong Kong people still refuse to be recognized as Chinese. When I came to the United States, I heard a lot of talk about the discrimination that exists here. My friends and family warned me I wouldn't make it in America because I was Asian and a woman. I never believed that. To me, the

United States is culturally diverse. In fact, I saw more races here than I had ever seen. When I was told my life would be difficult in the United States due to discrimination, I was even more determined to break that barrier.

Today, when I turn on cable news, I'm frustrated by the divisive language, which instills a dangerous mindset into people. We should focus on how to bridge differences and move forward, rather than categorizing each person as red or blue, left or right. We need to acknowledge how good America is and stop fighting with each other.

We are naturally drawn to others who share our socioeconomic status, religion, political beliefs, ethnicity, language, and gender. Even so, we must be careful about these innate preferences. My firsthand experience of how hatred and prejudice powered the Indonesia riot has made me more cognizant of this and has affected how I approach my business in America. As a result, I avoid ethnically driven organizations because I want to erase any divisive lines between organizations. I know how insidious these judgments can be. I am making a conscious decision to be inclusive and surround myself with others who share the same mindset.

CHAPTER SIX

CHOOSE YOUR OWN PATH

Once my mother and I safely landed in Manado after the riots, everything seemed to go back to normal, but psychologically, I wasn't the same. I often hid inside the bathroom crying. The only thing that brought me peace was having new friends who had also just returned to Manado from escaping these riots. The longer I waited for a response from universities, my hope for returning to the United States for school seem to dwindle because of the financial crisis in Asia, which made my tuition almost five times more expensive due to the currency depreciation. My parents tried to make me feel better by offering to buy me a car if I stayed to run the restaurant instead. They told me I wasn't a failure because a lot of other wealthier kids were coming back to Indonesia because of the economic crisis. My response was simply, "No way! I *will* go back to America. I'll work more. I'll figure it out." My parents never pushed me academically. In fact, they always told me to take a step back and not push myself so hard.

Unfortunately, I received a rejection letter from UCLA. I was devastated because that letter changed the entire trajectory of my life. As I sobbed in bed, my father asked why I *had* to go to UCLA instead of UC Irvine, which is also a reputable school. I told him I needed it on my résumé in order to find a good job. "This is for my future success," I explained. I was not going to accept the school's rejection without one more try. I worked hard on a letter of appeal, citing my performance in junior college, my volunteer work in several school clubs, and my work ethic, both at my parents' restaurant and during the school year. I implored them to give me another chance. I couldn't accept rejection unless I knew I had tried my best. I sent the letter off and waited.

The waiting became excruciating, so I decided to go to Hong Kong to stay with my sister. Like the rest of my family, she too was struggling financially. She was living on the fourth floor of an apartment with no elevator in a low-income area. It was a very small apartment with an extremely small bathroom inside the kitchen where cockroaches were often found. In order to avoid feeling claustrophobic, I spent my days walking the city while my sister worked. I checked the mail daily, and one day, there was a letter from UCLA. I opened it slowly. *This is it. This is my future.* "Congratulations," it read. I had been accepted! I screamed and jumped for joy. My sister tried to seem excited for me, but we both knew that my going back to the United States would put a major strain on my parents one more time.

SURROUND YOURSELF WITH THE RIGHT PEOPLE

After receiving my acceptance from UCLA, I flew back to the United States, but I didn't have a home anymore. My friend Rebecca had been living in Santa Monica in an apartment she shared with several other people. When she decided to move back in with her aunt, she offered me her room to rent. I was suddenly living with several strangers. The apartment was extremely old, and no matter how much we cleaned, the countertops and the carpets always felt sticky, like they had a permanent layer of grease on them.

Over the course of the school year, my roommates started moving out, one after another, leaving me to act as landlord and fill the rooms. I charged $350 for each of the upstairs bedrooms and $500 for the master bedroom. Each time a roommate gave me their notice, I'd post an ad on Craigslist. I created my own application form and sublease agreements with rules, including cleaning duties. I'd post online and get twenty or thirty responses. I had the idea to host an open house and let the potential renters come see the place. It wasn't until years later that I realized those were my first open houses. This became my first self-training in real estate. It didn't take long for me to realize that since I was handling the paying of utilities and filling the rooms, I could charge a little more rent and get my own monthly rent down to $100.

> IT WASN'T UNTIL YEARS LATER THAT I REALIZED THOSE WERE MY FIRST OPEN HOUSES. THIS BECAME MY FIRST SELF-TRAINING IN REAL ESTATE.

UCLA turned out to be much different than Santa Monica College. The campus was sprawling, the classes were huge, and I mostly felt lost amid the crowds. Even though this had been my dream for so long, I wasn't happy. The students were smart, and I felt intimidated by them. I thought about quitting. However, I knew if I quit, I'd regret it in the future.

I continued to struggle, even in a class I thought I'd be good at: business writing in Chinese. Since I was still dating my overbearing boyfriend who went to University of Irvine, I was too afraid to make new friends. I became timid and shy. My relationship with him continued to be abusive. His outbursts were explosive, and he often yelled and pushed me. He even dragged me across his apartment once. We fought a lot, but he always apologized afterward and explained how badly he felt. I started having dark and suicidal thoughts. I wondered why my life was so difficult, both financially and in a relationship. I felt alone and trapped. I thought coming to America was my escape from hardships, but I was learning that wasn't the case. I started cutting my wrists but stopped myself before I sliced too deep because I couldn't bear the thought of the heartache I'd cause my parents. I cried often and prayed that one day I might find peace and enjoy the comfort of a family and a home.

One day, my boyfriend accompanied me to the doctor for a cold, and the doctor noticed my wrists. She asked him to leave the room for privacy. He reluctantly did so. As soon as we were alone, she asked, "What's that?" I answered matter-of-factly, "Oh, sometimes when I fight with my boyfriend, I cut myself. It's nothing." She asked me how often I did that, and I laughed it off and told her I cut myself much less frequently now, only about once a month. She was taken aback. "Why are you staying with him if the anguish would cause you to have suicidal thoughts?" she asked. I wondered too. She left the room and came back with a piece of paper. It was a handwritten contract promising I would either call the suicide hotline or call her directly if I ever had any suicidal thoughts again. "I'd like for you to sign this, please." Honestly, I didn't think it was a big deal at the time, and I was surprised a stranger would care this much about me. To make her feel better, I flippantly signed it so she would stop questioning me, without any intention to ever call her.

One day, we fought again. But this time, instead of cutting myself, I drank a whole bottle of liquor. The heartbreak was so much that I wanted it to stop, so I took a couple of painkillers. I passed out in my bedroom. My boyfriend returned and found me unconscious beside the pill bottle. He immediately drove me to the ER. On the way, I started vomiting out the window while he was driving. I blacked out again, and when I awoke, I was lying on a hospital bed surrounded by nurses putting tubes down my throat. I wasn't able to talk. I had no idea, but they were pumping my stomach. When they took the tube out from my nose, I started bleeding. One of the hospital staff asked me, "Were you trying to kill yourself?" I was so groggy and ill, so I answered, "I don't know; I guess." Immediately a doctor said, "Admit her to the psychiatric ward!" I wanted to change my answer at that time, but it was too late.

STOP BEING A VICTIM

I was taken to the psychiatric ward where I was watched day and night. I felt locked up. They wouldn't let me leave. I had no privacy. There was a nurse beside me at all times. Only later did I realize that I was on suicide watch. I wondered how I got here. On April 20, 1999, I watched the news on the Columbine shooting while I was in the cafeteria for my scheduled meal. I was already so sad, and then watching the images on the TV made me sadder. The world just seemed so cruel to me, so dark. My whole body hurt. That's the thing about depression—it *hurts*. Your entire body and mind ache. I wanted to get out of there. I felt like I was in jail and being punished for being me.

After five days in the psychiatric ward, they released me to a psychiatrist. When she asked me if I thought I was depressed, I laughed. I told her I was only there because the doctors made me go. "This is so stupid," I told her. I guess she could sense I wasn't ready to talk, so she sent me home and told me to come back in two days. I didn't want to go back, but when I did, something in me had shifted. Almost before she could ask me anything, I started crying. The tears poured out of me. I told her about my struggles at UCLA—that I wasn't doing well academically and that my boyfriend and I often fought. She asked, "Why are you staying in this kind of relationship?" I told her I had grown to depend on him for rides to and from school and work. I told her about the riots in Indonesia; I was shaking as I replayed the horrific scenes in my head. She listened silently and then told me about the Anniversary Effect. She said that it's not unusual for a person to reexperience trauma during its anniversary. I realized it had been almost exactly a year since the riots. She quickly determined I was suffering from depression and prescribed me an antidepressant. I wondered during my walk home: Was I clinically depressed? Or was it just my experiences in life that caused my sadness? I refused to be labeled as a depressed patient and to rely on medication for the rest of my life based on one conversation with a psychiatrist. I decided it was my mindset that needed to be changed, not my brain chemistry. I threw the medicine away and took back control of my mindset.

Despite my reluctance to take the medication, her words had gotten through to me. I realized that I was sad because my relationship with my boyfriend was unhealthy. Not only did we fight, but he also often asked to borrow small amounts of money from me to pay for utility bills. Although it was never more than $50, it was significant, as that would be almost all of the money I had in my bank account. I thought back to my parents telling me never to loan money to friends (like they had done) without putting it in writing. So I asked him to sign a promissory note listing the amount borrowed, interest rate, and the date the repayment would be made. But my recent hospital visit made me think harder about our dynamic. We were in the car when I told him I could no longer loan him money, and he started yelling and driving erratically. Suddenly something in me clicked: "This is it. I cannot be with you anymore!" I wish it could have been a clean break, but our "breaking up" was ugly and lasted several more unfortunate months. But I was no longer labeled the victim, the abused, the depressed patient. I was free.

ETHICS AND HARD WORK TRUMP EASY MONEY

Not long after we officially broke up, a new guy showed up. (Some lessons are harder to learn than others!) He was charming and came from a religious and wealthy family. We didn't have dramatic fights like my last relationship, so I relaxed into a healthier dynamic, as I thought. I was working several jobs at this point, and he did not work. This large discrepancy in lifestyle started to become a strain on us. It made me resentful to be working so hard to get by while he did nothing and had money to spare. He would get a new fancy Audi and then a few weeks later start begging his parents for a new BMW. Instead of working hard to earn his new cars, he wrote letters to the auto dealerships claiming he got lemons, so they would give him a new car. Then, as he was failing school, he stole my hospital paperwork and submitted it to the dean, claiming he had been diagnosed with cancer. He convinced the dean to give him a full letter grade higher than he'd earned. I started seeing a pattern in how he lied to get what he wanted, a trait of a pathological liar.

Meanwhile, I was tired of asking him for rides to work, class, and the library. Clearly, our focuses were different. I wanted a car, but being a foreign student, I didn't have enough credit history to lease a car. The only car dealership that was willing to lease to me based on my credit history was Oldsmobile; however, I didn't have proof of income. I assured them by explaining about my three jobs and my determination to find a good job once I graduated from college. They agreed. Back at the university, kids often laughed. "An Asian girl driving an Oldsmobile!" I, however, was so proud of myself, and I drove that car with my head held high.

Now that I had my own car, I also started two unpaid internships, with Merrill Lynch and Salomon Brothers, respectively. Many people who saw me struggling financially asked me why I would take an unpaid internship. My answer was always that the experiences were invaluable and could build my résumé. At Merrill Lynch, I learned how to conduct research and gather data from different platforms. I also helped consultants find active mergers and acquisitions. At Salomon Brothers, I learned to do cold calling, which was so vital to me in my early years in real estate. I did not enjoy it, but I learned technique, and I learned to speak English in a professional and confident manner. Despite my accent, I was the top caller among the other interns. Those were the rewards of the experiences, and I still rely on them today.

Despite my long days of work and school, it was worth it to have the freedom my car afforded me. On one outing, my "wealthy" boyfriend and I drove separately, and when we stopped for gas, he jumped out and offered to pay, which was unusual. I got out of the car and saw him with a credit card. "Can I see your card?" I asked.

He refused. I ended up snatching it from him and saw another person's name on the card. He admitted he had found the card on the street. He had essentially stolen someone's money! I refused to let him use it and hopped into my car and drove to his house. I told his mother what he'd done and hoped she would see the wrong of this. He came into the house behind me and started kicking me *in front of his mother*. I loved his mother, but I was furious she didn't do enough to raise him to be an ethical person despite their wealth. I broke up with him that day. It was another long and painful breakup, but from these relationships, I learned to stand up for myself and never give in to the "easy life" in order to let good things happen to me.

> I LEARNED TO STAND UP FOR MYSELF AND NEVER GIVE IN TO THE "EASY LIFE" IN ORDER TO LET GOOD THINGS HAPPEN TO ME.

During all of the tumultuous relationships, I still had to keep up with my schoolwork. It wasn't easy, but I managed to graduate in 2000. My father flew in from Indonesia, and my sister flew in from Hong Kong; it was their first time in the United States. My mother could not afford to come along, so she stayed back to work. We all stayed in my tiny bedroom, and it was emotional to show them my new life here in the United States. After I walked and received my diploma on stage, I hugged my dad for a long time, and he whispered, "I am so proud of you." We both wept. This was a momentous time because we knew each of us had struggled silently on our own in three different countries for many years, but we had gotten through it.

My father and I at my UCLA graduation. This was his first time in the United States.

My overwhelming feeling at graduation was relief. I thought, *Finally I'm done burdening my parents.* I knew that having an economics degree from UCLA meant I could go out and take charge of my life. This was the moment I had worked so hard for. When I was little, I used to tell my parents I would go to school in America and make enough money to support them. On the day I received my student visa to come to the United States, I told my dad, "Give me ten years, and I'll buy you a Ferrari." Even today, he will still ask me jokingly, "Where's my Ferrari?" I just look at him and smile and say, "You're too old to drive a Ferrari now."

ADVICE ON HAVING A HEALTHY MINDSET

During my time at UCLA, I spent many hours wondering why I stayed in unhealthy relationships for so long. What I realized was that both partners were romantic and kind in the beginning. Maybe *too* romantic and *too* kind? What people outside of dysfunctional relationships don't get is that when the relationship is good, it's *really* good. I always think of Korean dramas with their romantic stories of angst and desire. I think these art forms blur the lines between tragedy and love and can confuse the understanding of courtship. At the time, I thought all relationships were like mine. I didn't want to be alone, so I thought these were as good as it got. I have since learned that healthy relationships allow and encourage space for both partners. Healthy partnerships are built by healthy individuals. You must know your own boundaries so that others don't cross them and snatch your life away from you. When a person's freedoms are limited, so is their happiness. True, healthy love allows you room to grow and evolve into your full potential.

CHAPTER SEVEN

TAKE CONTROL

My sister and father continued to stay with me for a month after graduation. It was fun showing them around, but mostly they accompanied me to my many job interviews. I applied for over fifty jobs, so I had several interviews a week. There was a lot of prep work, considering there was no GPS at that time, so I had to map out my routes between locations. I had been practicing interviews at the UCLA Career Center, and most of my interviews were promising up until the moment I mentioned I needed a company sponsorship for a work (H1B) visa. I was racing against time since my status had changed from an F1 student visa to an Optional Practical Training (OPT), which gave me one year to transition into an H1B work visa; otherwise, I would be headed back to Asia. Time after time

I heard, "Sorry, we don't sponsor." I finally decided I needed to change my technique. Remembering the saying that asking for forgiveness is easier than asking for permission, I decided to get a job offer *before* I mentioned my need for sponsorship.

After countless hours driving and interviewing, I did land a job as an administrative assistant at a start-up internet company. They offered me a $32,000 salary and a sponsorship. I felt rich. I was elated. By this time, my sister and father had left, so I put all of my energy into my new job. I worked in an all-male sales department. I was comfortable working in the department not looking like everyone else, and I did not feel I was beneath everyone else because I was an administrative assistant. Rather, I thought I could finally build some new friendships after two overbearing relationships. However, I soon realized I was never invited to lunch breaks with everyone else. The familiar feeling of being left out returned. The thought of quitting returned. However, right before Christmas, the company announced a massive layoff that included me. I was relieved; I was even offered a two months' severance package. With even less time to spare until my OPT expired, I immediately started my job hunting again.

I desperately applied for any jobs available. At several of these interviews, I was provided different personality tests. I was told over and over again that my test results indicated that I'd be a perfect advisor, consultant, or salesperson. I could hardly understand the logic, as I despised the notion of going into sales. Why would I work so hard to graduate from a college and become a salesperson? Finally I interviewed with a pension consulting firm in Santa Monica as an analyst. This sounded much more sophisticated and could also qualify me for the H1B visa. After five rounds of interviews, I was offered a salary starting at $36,000. Not only were they willing to help me with my H1B visa application, but it also was a five-minute drive from my Santa Monica apartment. I also had a window that overlooked the Pacific Ocean, and I often imagined my parents on the other side of that wide ocean. "Look at me, Mommy and Daddy! Are you proud of me?" I stared at those blue waters every day and felt connected to home.

During peak time, I'd work till past midnight to rush out our institutional clients' analysis performance reports on time. I worked alongside other analysts, and we developed amazing friendships that have lasted until today. We hung out most days and nights, enjoying our social lives, and this time was a highlight of my twenties. I never had solid friends in college because of my overbearing boyfriends. This robbed me of the traditional carefree college experience of partying. Now, for the first time in my life, I felt free and finally felt happy! At the end of my first year, I was given a five-star performance review, so I was offered the highest

> **FOR THE FIRST TIME IN MY LIFE, I FELT FREE AND FINALLY FELT HAPPY!**

percentage raise our department was allowed to give: 5 percent. I left the office excited! I did the math and realized that was merely $150 increase per month, *before* tax. Regardless, I was happy.

In 2002, my mother finally came to visit. I was so excited to show her around and spend every minute together. She was part of my everyday life for the first time in six years. I was living in a simple apartment with makeshift cardboard boxes I had collected from behind supermarkets as closet shelving. With my mother's help, we decided to decorate my bedroom. I took her to IKEA, which she found fascinating. She said, "In Asia, you just buy it and take it home. In America, you must assemble it yourself." My sister joined us a few days later, and I proudly drove them around in my Oldsmobile Alero.

My mother and I enjoying her first trip to the United States

IT'S OK TO BE ALONE

Within six years in the United States, I had been in two relationships that were abusive, possessive, or overbearing. I could not accept that any relationship should be this way. I decided that I would stay single for an entire year to meet different people and figure out what I needed from a partnership. After work one day, my coworkers and I were headed to our usual hangout in the famous Korea Town. My coworker David mentioned he had an old friend who had just graduated from the Naval Academy and would be joining the US Marine Corps shortly. He told us he'd invited him to meet up with us. When the friend arrived, we were all introduced. His name was John, and he took the seat across from me. I remember my girlfriend leaned over to me and whispered, "Ooh, he's pretty cute." He *was* cute, but he was quiet. In fact, he just mostly sat there expressionless. I decided to be friendly and initiate a conversation. I asked him how old he was. He answered curtly that he was twenty-two. I was twenty-four at the time, and I remember thinking, *He's so young!*

When John called me a few days later, he explained that he had gotten my phone number from my coworker. He was nice, but I told him bluntly that I wasn't interested in dating. *I'm taking the year off,* I thought. I told him I'd be happy to go to dinner with him as friends, but that was all. He accepted, and we went to dinner that weekend, and it was … quiet. Very quiet. He was nice but was nothing like the guys I was drawn to. There was no spark, romance, drama, passion. In fact, there was nothing but scant conversation.

During my months as a single girl, I decided to put my analyst skills to good use to figure out the kind of guy I wanted, so naturally, I built a spreadsheet. In it, I included every character trait I wanted my ideal partner to possess. There were over twenty, and for each one, I designated a point value. For example, *He has to be a family man—ten points. He needs to like cats—five points.* Then I listed all the guys I had met, including ex-boyfriends and male friends I wasn't romantically interested in. I scored every person to see which one met my criteria. Needless to say, it was a long spreadsheet.

I included John on the spreadsheet, but his score was low; he clearly was not the man for me. Even so, he continued to call me every Wednesday. Several weeks had gone by when he invited me to be his date at the Marine Birthday Ball. I said no immediately. After all, he was a low scorer, and my analytics were ironclad, so it would clearly never work. John said he knew we were just friends, and that he thought we would have fun since it was held in Las Vegas. He was persistent, and he told me he would not take no for an answer. So I finally agreed to go.

When the day of the ball arrived, John showed up in his old faded T-shirt and outdated jeans in a ten-year-old Honda Accord with broken AC. I borrowed a dress from my friend and told John he should drive us in my leased Oldsmobile to Las Vegas instead. The drive there was pretty boring. Shocker! I already regretted coming. When we got to the hotel, he hopped out of the car, grabbed his stuff, and headed toward the hotel. He left everything else for me to grab myself. I sighed and thought, *Jeez, this guy is horrible.*

Once we got dressed, we met with a couple of his friends and had a glass of wine. I relaxed, and John seemed more relaxed too. We started having fun, and his friends were lively and friendly. This was the first time I had ever been to a military event, and it was exhilarating. Despite how young they all looked, I could sense their pride wearing their blues. We ended up having a nice time, and I was glad I'd gone.

The next morning, we woke up late and made it to the breakfast buffet just in time. John went back to being quiet. *Again with this man!* I was used to guys trying to win me over, but it seemed like John didn't care if I was there or not. After I grabbed some food and sat down to eat, I became more uncomfortable and angrier for being there. I was so relieved when the trip was over.

John continued to call me and asked me on a date to San Diego to meet some of his friends. I don't know why, but I said yes, as I figured he was harmless. His friends were loud and fun. I had a strong Long Island iced tea and suddenly felt emboldened enough to say, "I want to be up front with you. I don't think you know how to be a gentleman and treat a girl properly. I will never be your girl-friend." His response was, "We'll see."

For the next few weeks, he continued to call and drove over seventy miles to visit me every week. During this time, there were talks of an Iraq invasion, but no details were ever given. In January 2003, my coworker David told me that John was leaving for Iraq in a few days. *What?* I panicked. I knew we weren't dating and that I didn't want to be his girlfriend—after all, my spreadsheet confirmed that he was not my man—yet the news of him going to war deeply affected me. It seemed to be happening so fast. We went out for one last night with David and our friends. He left a couple of days later, and I did not know when I would hear from him again.

On Valentine's Day, I received a bouquet of flowers and a card from him. The note said, "Hey, I'll be thinking of you while I'm in the Middle East." I was so touched, but I had no way to thank him. He had prepared this before he left for the war. A few days later, I received a handwritten letter from him, so I wrote back. Each time, he'd write back, and we continued our penpalship. His were always handwritten in a small envelope, and they detailed what he spent his time doing—like cleaning his rifle and spending time with his marines. He always asked what I had been up to, so I always typed up my letters detailing all the fun things I had been doing in the United States.

One day in August, I received an email from him, "I'm now in Kuwait. How are you doing? Thanks for not writing back." Turned out, he had never received any of my letters, but he continued to write me anyway to keep his own spirits up. We exchanged a few more emails daily. One day David came to my cubicle and said, "Hey, I just had lunch with John." I froze, and my heart started pounding. I was upset he did not tell me, but just then John walked over from behind my cubicle wall, and seeing him safe and whole melted my heart.

To celebrate his return, we decided to go to a fancy bowling alley club in Hollywood. We agreed to go home, wash up, and meet up at the alley. At home, I changed outfits and did my hair and makeup. I met my friends at the bowling alley, but John wasn't there yet. When he showed up with a few military buddies, he was once again wearing an old, wrinkled T-shirt, shorts, and flip-flops. I said, "They let you in like this?"

"What do you mean?" he answered. I thought to myself, *I can't believe this guy is trying to date me dressed like that!* It was clear to me again that this guy was wrong for me, and I had the analytics—and the questionable wardrobe choices—to prove it.

TIME WILL TELL

John and I spent more time together after he returned from Iraq. As winter grew closer, my year of being single was up. I didn't feel I was that much closer to cracking the code of "my guy." John had asked me to be his girlfriend, but I told him we should still stay friends and take things slowly. He was fine with that, and he never rushed me into making a decision. I had promised myself that the next time I committed, it would be to someone I'd consider marrying. Five months after his return, I started to admire how calm and steady he was. He was authentic and passionate about his work. The time we spent together was peaceful and unlike the time I had spent with previous boyfriends. Then, it hit me: *Oh my God, he is the one*! I realized that my spreadsheet was skewed. I hadn't even realized the integral traits that I'd been missing, like feeling relaxed, steady, and secure around a person. There was no drama with John, so I had equated that with having no passion. Was my entire spreadsheet faulty?

In January, I told him I was now ready to be his girlfriend. He answered, "I thought you wanted to be just friends?" I was mortified: "Is that what you want? For us to remain friends?" I was getting frustrated. *"I did want to be friends, but now I want you to ask me to be your girlfriend!"* He smiled, as if he knew all along it would end this way. He asked, and I accepted. It was January 17, 2004, and after knowing him for fifteen months, moving at the slowest pace I have ever allowed myself to get to know a person, I had found my man. He is Korean, but he wasn't the hero from a Korean drama, for sure. He wasn't romantic, but he also wasn't dramatic. He said what he meant. He was thoughtful and calm, even during disagreements. It was unlike any relationship I had ever seen or experienced. I realized that the greatest gifts from a partner weren't flowers or jewelry—they were respectful discourse and loving concern.

After my proclamation, we started *really* dating. I still lived in Santa Monica; he was based in Camp Pendleton, which was a little over a hundred miles away. The drive took over three hours with traffic, but we saw each other every week. We continued to get closer, and I fell deeply in love. I was happy until he told me he had volunteered to go to Ramadi, Iraq, to replace a team of soldiers who had just been killed. I dropped to the floor and begged him, "Why? Why would you volunteer?" He just said, "Because I need to be there with my brothers."

Just a couple of days later, along with his parents and his brother, we drove to the airport. He knew I hated airports, and this time would be no different. He told us, "Don't get out of the car. Just drop me off." When he shut the door, his mother and I clung to one another and cried. I didn't even know his family well at the time, but this was surely a bonding moment for us. We were all sharing the same love and pain for John.

Though I was still working at the pension consulting firm, it was hard to concentrate because I was so sad and scared with John away. My friends didn't really understand my pain. I don't think they realized how much I cared for him at that point. A group of coworkers started running after work, and I joined them. I had never been a runner, but John was, so running made me feel closer to him.

While I ran, I thought about our relationship. How was it so easy for him to leave? I decided to let him know how I was feeling in a letter. By this time, the military had established a system in Iraq where my emails could be printed and delivered to wherever his platoon was located. In it, I questioned his intentions and whether my feelings were reciprocated. In his reply, he told me our relationship was the last thing he thought of and suggested that we ought to take a break. I was furious—after all, the man I thought I could marry did not feel the same for me. I was devastated and stopped writing him back. He called me three weeks later from a satellite phone, and I hesitantly picked up. He told me he had received my care package and he missed hearing from me. He apologized for suggesting a break. We talked until the satellite phone lost its signal, and I fell even more deeply in love.

He was away for seven months, and during that time I logged many miles trying to outrun my fear for his safety. I sent care packages to him and avoided watching the news. When he returned in October, I waited with his family at the base for over five hours. When the soldiers marched out, I could not control my tears.

Months after he returned, I reminded him how much he had hurt me when he asked for a break while he was in Iraq. He looked at me and explained, "Babe, I was in a Humvee every day guiding my driver and leading my marines in the back. If I had been distracted by my personal life for even one second, I could have driven over an IED and risked my marines' lives. I asked for a break because I had to focus and protect my marines." I was speechless. How could I have been so selfish and ignorant? While I was worrying about myself, my own feelings, and my own future, he was putting the lives of his marines before his own. This made me love him even more.

EVERYTHING HAPPENS FOR A GOOD REASON

In December 2004, I decided to take my annual leave to spend my first Christmas in nine years with my family. Before I left the United States, I made sure I had all the required documentation to return. I was still holding a H1B visa status sponsored by the pension consulting firm; I requested my original H1B visa approval letter from my company and made a few copies as backup.

First I arrived in Indonesia and spent a lovely holiday with my parents. Then, I went to Hong Kong to see my sister, and I had to report at the US Embassy for my visa stamp to return to the United States. However, at the embassy, they pointed to my documents and said, "This is not the original visa approval letter." I countered, "I must have given you one of my backup copies," but none of the pages I showed them was the original. They said I must have photocopied a photocopy, *not* the original. I panicked. I knew my company had to have the original. I contacted my coworkers in the United States to help locate the document, but the manager who originally helped me with the approval had since left the company. The new manager had no idea where my document could be. Ultimately, the embassy rejected my requests. Because of one missing paper, I was not allowed to return to America. The American Dream life that I had built was crumbling right in front of my eyes.

I called John crying. I couldn't believe that I had finally found a good man, a good job, and good friends, and it was being taken from me because someone misplaced a piece of paper. Did they not know what that paper meant for me? John was trying to help me by asking all of his friends and family if they had any connections who could help me get back. In the meantime, I begged the HR department at my company to produce any documentation that could help me get back. During this time, the company had just laid off a lot of workers, although my position was safe. You know who your true friends are during the difficult times. I had a few coworkers who helped me daily to speak with the management and HR to find my paperwork, though others tried to stay away from the "trouble." All I needed was evidence to prove that I was employed by the company, and hopefully I could ask the embassy to produce another approval letter. Suddenly, the CEO of the company ordered my friends to stop assisting me, or their employment would be threatened. HR started accusing me for working under an illegal status. Everyone stopped helping me and answering my emails. My manager simply told me, "I'm so sorry. I really want to help you, but you're not here, and several people want your job. Since we don't know when you're coming back, we are instructed not to hold your position for you any longer." I was devastated. Not only had I devoted so much of my energy at this company, but they also disowned me when I needed them the most. After all these years, all this work, all this effort, I was right back where I started—in Hong Kong, alone. Everything I painstakingly had built since 1996 was gone. I couldn't even go back to get my belongings.

AFTER ALL THESE YEARS, ALL THIS WORK, ALL THIS EFFORT, I WAS RIGHT BACK WHERE I STARTED—IN HONG KONG, ALONE.

John relentlessly explored different channels and asked for help through different relationships. Each time we thought we had found a solution, something else would happen and take me back to where I first started. I thought maybe John and I were not meant to be. God wanted me to stay back in Hong Kong somehow.

I decided to go back to the US Embassy and apply for a tourist visa as a last resort. It may seem like a simple idea, but everyone told me they would never grant me a tourist visa due to my visa problem. I went to the embassy feeling less hopeful than I'd ever been. When I talked to the embassy interviewer, I told him everything that had happened. I cried and my tears poured out uncontrollably: "I have all my personal belongings there. My entire life is there. Please give me a tourist visa so I can go back to pack up everything." I was shaking, and the harder I tried to hold back my tears, the more they came out. The interviewer wouldn't look at me. I could tell he felt bad. He said, "I'll approve your tourist visa, and you will have six months to pack up and come back." He gave me the stamp. I couldn't believe he was letting me go back. With one stamp, this man was allowing me to go back and possibly get my life back!

By now, it was February 2005. I immediately started packing. I couldn't wait to get back to the home I had grown to love and to John, the man I had fallen deeply in love with. When I landed in LA, John was there to pick me up. Having almost been separated from him again, and having him stand by me every day, fighting for my return and never giving up on me, I knew he was the only person I could trust and rely on. I knew without any doubt that John was the man I wanted to marry. We talked a lot about our future in the days after I returned. We knew that John would be leaving for Iraq in a few months. I knew I wanted to marry him, but I didn't know if he felt the same. When I explained to him that I only wanted to marry someone who knew I was "their person," he admitted that I was. We decided that we would file for a marriage certificate and that after he returned from his third tour, we would have a "real" wedding with family and friends.

We discussed our plan with his parents over dinner at a restaurant one night. By this time, we had spent more time separated in different countries than we had been together since we started seeing each other. John's mother trusted our decision, and John's father said, "I have faith in you. Don't disappoint us, OK?" With that, on February 28, 2005, John and I went to city hall in our old T-shirts and jeans to file for our marriage certificate. We decided to make this day as routine as possible so that our future ceremony would mean more. We swore in front of an officiant, and as much as I wanted to preserve this moment for our actual wedding, I knew then that he was my husband for life. I couldn't wait to have the wedding to formalize our marriage with the world.

Right after our city hall marriage, we rushed out to get my green card application. I was determined that despite our "marriage," I would remain financially independent and find my own way to the American Dream, as I had planned when I first came to the country. I refused to rely on John in any financial way. I told John I would wait for the day of our wedding, when we would share that special moment with our family and friends, to call him my husband officially.

Six months after our city hall marriage, John was readying to leave for his third tour to Iraq. He filled out his military paperwork and said, "In case something happens to me while I am in Iraq, they need to notify somebody. You are my wife now, so I have to put your name down." I said, "No, no, no, I can't do this. I cannot handle this." He replied calmly, "Well, you have to, because we're married." When John was around, he gave me a sense of security. When he was gone, I was terrified.

Early one foggy morning, I joined my in-laws at the Camp Pendleton base to send him off. I stayed stronger this time, or at least I appeared to be. John needed us to give him a quick and joyful goodbye, so that's what I did. He turned and walked away with conviction.

When John walked away for his third deployment

Even though he told me he would call me on the satellite phone as soon as he arrived in Iraq, I didn't hear from him for weeks. I started burying myself at work because I was afraid if I went home, somebody would be standing at the door waiting for me with bad news about John. Finally, he called. I asked what took him so long to call. "We only have a certain amount of time to use the phone. I'm the captain, so I let all my marines use it first. They needed to contact their families." That was the kind of person and leader he was. I was proud to call him my husband.

When he came home from his third tour, he *formally* proposed. We flew back to Manado together so my parents could meet him for the first time. Even though they could not understand English, they knew John was the right person for me. They embraced him immediately and introduced him to the rest of the family.

We threw a frugal wedding by focusing on our guests rather than the decor. Our wedding was so much fun, and it was a greater experience than I could have ever imagined. After we got married, I told John about my spreadsheet, which had depicted him as an unfit partner for me. We laughed about his pitifully low score. He looked at me and said, "Remember when you said you would never be my girlfriend?" I told him of course I remembered. He smiled. "Well, you were right. You became my wife instead."

ADVICE ON MAKING CHOICES

Life is full of decisions. Some seem small at the time only to prove to be pivotal later. Others carry gravity from the beginning. In order to make sound decisions—whether major or minor—you must lead with your personal values. When you make choices based on greed or selfish motivations, you are not following your authentic path. If you are choosing a partner, for example, take your time and find someone who allows you the freedom to be yourself. If you are making a business decision, find people whose ethics align with your own so that you are positioned for the kind of success and fortune you can be proud of.

CHAPTER EIGHT

CRISIS MEETS OPPORTUNITY

危機

The word *crisis* in Chinese is 危機, composed of two words: danger and opportunity. My mother always told me that in every crisis, opportunities exist. The risks, she claimed, brought added rewards. In fact, my mom—always an example of cunning resourcefulness—grossed her highest earnings during the 1998 Asian financial crisis. Though my parents' restaurant in Indonesia was losing money at the time, she saw an opportunity to make up for lost revenue by purchasing raw materials—like sugar, soap, and cloves—with Indonesian currency. Because inflation throughout Asia was so bad, people from other countries would buy her inventory, and my mother would accept foreign currency instead.

She wasn't scared by the risks of the recession; she was only emboldened by the potential rewards. My mother's example of ingenuity and creativity amid chaos ended up helping me through some of the hardest crises of my own life.

After we signed our initial marriage paperwork in 2005, I started applying for jobs again and got an offer from Sony. Before I accepted, I recalled my time at the pension firm when I had worked as an analyst for huge corporations and their pension fund portfolios. I remember how the stock market plunged by as much as 80 percent due to the internet bubble bust in 2002. Not only did a lot of hardworking teachers and government workers lose their pensions, but they also lost their jobs. I thought to myself, *What if I work for a firm and rely on their pension, only to lose my savings and my job?* It was very tempting to accept the job offer at Sony with a paycheck within a month and work for such a reputable company. But I decided I needed to take better control of my future. Should I accept the analyst position or follow my gut? I decided I had never been cowardly before, so why start now?

I started attending free real estate investment seminars. These were pivotal experiences for me because I found myself there. Not only was I learning new things in the classes, but I discovered a sense of purpose. I had struggled with confidence for so many years, and suddenly I was empowered. The facilitators reminded us often that we were worthy and powerful. My heart would race as I sat in the audience, soaking up every new insight I could. There was motivation to excel, learn more, do better—I felt like I had found my tribe. I met a lot of new people and was amassing quite a collection

THERE WAS MOTIVATION TO EXCEL, LEARN MORE, DO BETTER—I FELT LIKE I HAD FOUND MY TRIBE.

of business cards. After each conversation, I sent the person a nice email, reminding them of where we met, how we met, and even some of the discussions we shared. I started grouping these contacts and eventually created a database of investors I knew were interested in real estate.

However, I was lost in the real estate world, and I was too timid to begin my real estate investing career. I came across an ad for a mortgage loan officer position. I knew I was good with numbers, so it seemed like a good fit. I was hired almost immediately and became a mortgage loan officer. I spent hours learning about different mortgage products, like option ARMs (adjustable-rate mortgages) and subprime mortgages. I was told to find business by cold calling, and I was given pages of phone numbers to dial. I was excited, as I had learned how to cold call when I interned at Salomon Brothers. But landing a client and closing the deal is much more difficult that it seemed, and after three months, I still hadn't made any money.

My parents were worried about me, but I was so excited to share the knowledge I had gained. "In America, you don't need a down payment to buy a house!" They couldn't believe that was possible. I didn't necessarily know what it all meant, but I was learning what the lenders had shared with us. Different account executives from different banks came in every day and taught us how to sell their mortgage products that yielded the most "rebate"—a fee that mortgage brokers earn from selling the bank's products. The subprime products and option ARMS produced the most rebates, so our managing broker told us to sell those.

At the time, the company was led by a beautiful twenty-nine-year-old female broker, who was an immigrant, and her very handsome American husband. I admired what she had built as an immigrant. Soon, though, I started to see *how* she built this for herself using poor practices and how she led the loan officers. She taught us to charge clients the maximum amount of fees allowed by law by using creative terms on the good-faith estimate. She also later called me into her office and encouraged me to use my "feminism" to gain more business. "Let me show you," she said, batting her eyes and smiling flirtatiously, as she did when meeting a male prospect. When I realized this company was led by such low ethics, I decided to leave. I spoke with three coworkers, and we joined another mortgage brokerage firm and leased a tiny office space close to downtown LA. I was gaining a lot of experience, but I wasn't making as much money as I was hoping.

Two and a half years after I had started working as a mortgage loan officer, the mortgage industry collapsed due to poor loan products that set up many homeowners for failure. My real estate career was collapsing also. My savings dwindled, and I had acquired tens of thousands of dollars in credit card debt. I wondered if maybe I was wrong to pursue a real estate career in the first place.

OVERCOMING OBSTACLES

Since leaving my pension consulting firm, I had wanted to get into real estate investing, but I never had the confidence or the money. My hope was that these classes might give me the strategies I needed to break into the investment world. In one seminar, we discussed how to buy property with no money down and receive cash back at closing. This sounded too good to be true, but this was exactly the kind of information I sought. I decided to heed my mother's advice and unearth my opportunity by taking action to begin looking for my first real estate investment property.

After doing some research, I found a newspaper ad that listed a duplex in Dallas, Texas, for $115,000. At a previous conference, I learned about the 1 percent rule: the monthly rent should be at least 1 percent of the purchase price of the property. The Dallas property ad listed the rental amount at $1,200, which met the 1 percent criteria. I was thrilled. I called the listing agent to ask some questions. Honestly, I didn't know what questions to ask, but after speaking with him for a bit, I decided to make an offer.

From my past experience, I realized I never let obstacles block my path. I would keep finding other ways when I hit one. My first real estate investment was no different. In 2007, I decided to start the buying process and deal with any barriers as they arose. I found a loan officer who offered a zero-percent-down, stated income, stated asset product, which means the bank does not require any provable income.

One barrier was telling my husband about this investment. I told him about my plan, and after a series of discussions, he took a chance on me. Since I didn't have a job then, he let me apply for loans using his employment. Hiring the listing agent as my agent, I proceeded buying this property in Dallas, Texas, a place I had never even been.

In a previous seminar, I had learned that buying a property unseen requires a third party to be your eyes. To this end, I started building my team on the ground. I hired an inspector to visit the duplex and tell me what was bad and what was good. As he relayed his inspection report, it was a jumble of words; I had no context for what any of it meant, so I asked the listing agent for advice. What he told me was that the property wasn't too bad, and many of its issues could be fixed.

I asked for credits from the seller to pay for the needed repairs. The seller agreed. I was floored. Not only did I not put any money down, but I also got $6,000 back at closing. This was my first investment property purchase, and it was thrilling. After the closing, I was so proud of myself for learning everything from free seminars and taking this one bold step toward financial freedom.

I wish the story ended here with my rosy accomplishment, but in fact, it was just the beginning of a tumultuous process. After I bought the duplex, I learned that the listing brokerage firm could also manage the property for me. Initially, I was pleased with the convenient one-stop-shop service. However, within weeks, renters moved out one after another, and we were told both units required much more work than we had been informed during the purchase. I realized the serious consequences created by the clouded judgements of the broker due to the conflict of interest, by acting as our property manager as well as a dual agent, thus representing both the sellers and myself in the transaction. I scrambled to look for another property manager. Not long after we settled with a new one, I received a phone call alerting me that the police had raided the property because there were drug dealers and squatters on my property. I was overwhelmed with never-ending issues from this property, so I repeated what I had learned in my conferences inside my head: "Just make sure the property is clean, safe, and functional." With this manageable expectation in mind, our new property manager, who was also the contractor, replaced the floors with tile, fixed everything that was leaking, and replaced the appliances with used ones. Now that I had overcome these barriers, I had to get the units rented as quickly as possible.

As an out-of-state investor using the listing agent to represent me, I was not informed and had overlooked many details. His dual agency or dual commission had clouded his judgment to protect me as his client also. Not only had we bought in a bad area, which my agent had not informed me of, but I also wasn't aware of how badly deteriorated the property really was. In addition, there was a metal spiral staircase in each unit. Most potential renters took one look at the stairs and decided they didn't want the hassle of moving furniture up them. How had I overlooked this detail, and what was I going to do about it? Why didn't my agent mention this to me? I kept spending money on the units, but I had no rent coming in. It was starting to feel like I had found a crisis rather than an opportunity.

Only a few short weeks later, I received another call about the property: there had been a shooting in the neighborhood. I remember calling my husband to tell him. He replied angrily, "I'm so done with this property!" In that moment, I felt so disappointed in myself. What did I get us into? Why hadn't the listing agent told me the neighborhood was bad, the property was bad, the stairs were bad? I vowed to not fall prey to another greedy agent next time—if there ever was a next time.

I had to figure out a way to make this right. I was in crisis, and I had to find the opportunities that surely were hidden there. I didn't turn the crisis around overnight, but after five different property managers and more than three years of hard work, I finally got the property stabilized. In fact, I still own the property today, and it has become one of the easiest properties I own. Despite the hardships I endured and the mistakes I made in securing it, this Dallas property is my real estate baby. It was the first investment property I ever bought, and I did so using my own creative resourcefulness.

SCARY FIRSTS

After John returned from his third military tour, he was stationed at Camp Pendleton. At first, we decided he would commute to the base as needed from my apartment. After only a week of commuting, John said it was taking him too long to make the drive and that we needed a new living arrangement closer to his base. While I was building my real estate career, I was also working several part-time gigs to make ends meet—I had gone back to my college waitressing job, worked part time as an administrative assistant for a financial company, played extra roles for TV shows, and accepted modeling work. John wanted to buy his first home midway between his work and my Santa Monica home.

I started looking online and found a condominium halfway between Camp Pendleton and Santa Monica. The condo was one thousand square feet with two bedrooms and two baths and was listed at $499,000. It sounded perfect. I didn't know the area well, but when I went to look at it, it seemed nice. The unit itself had old carpet and needed updating, but I knew we could do that ourselves. We made an offer and bought it with 5 percent down payment.

I took over the remodeling projects of the new condo with zest. With an agreed-upon $15,000 budget, we painted, remodeled the bathrooms, and updated the entire kitchen and flooring. When the work was completed, the condo looked modern and sleek. Friends came over for our housewarming party, and I proudly escorted them through the unit, basking in their adulation.

This was my first remodeling project in my portfolio. Eventually, I moved out of my Santa Monica apartment and moved into our new condo. But I couldn't give up my low rent, so I decided to sublease my room and received $400 positive cash flow every month.

By this time, I had bought our first investment property and our first home. I was still convinced that real estate investment could change my life, so I continued attending investment seminars relentlessly. I signed up for a three-day Multiple Streams of Income conference offered by Robert Allen, a renowned real estate investment coach. I was invigorated by his positive messages and thrilled to learn his investing concepts. I went home after the first day and told my husband all about what I'd learned. I told him I wanted to try out Allen's boot camp, but it cost $15,000. I had a strong feeling that this would change my life, but I needed John's blessing on this. I knew that once I paid my enrollment costs with my own credit cards, I would still have to pay for flights and hotels for the various places we would visit. I believed I was paying for something valuable, and it would eventually pay off. John remained doubtful but finally said that if I felt strongly about this, he would support the expense. He said, "If you do this, learn all you can, and treat it as a college tuition and make it worthwhile." I remember crying and saying, "Yes, yes, yes" over and over. I felt deeply that this was going to be my turning point.

The next day of the conference, I returned with my credit card. When I handed it to one of the coaches, I was in tears, pleading, "This *has* to work. I need this so badly to break the bad luck I've had all my life. I can't afford this, but I'm trusting you." He assured me that the strategies would work if I applied them correctly. Once I paid the tuition, I went into research mode. I took furious notes on all the creative strategies they were teaching. I asked many questions. I told one of the coaches about the property I had bought in Texas. He started shaking his head and said that the deal sounded problematic, and he would have discouraged me from buying it: "It's OK. We'll teach you the right way so that next time you don't make the same mistakes." *Next time*, I repeated. I couldn't wait for next time.

During the coaching series, we were offered the opportunity to attend a "field trip" in Indianapolis, Atlanta, or Kansas City. I chose to work with a mentor named Gary who once mentioned that he bought properties in Kansas City, so that was my choice as well. Before the field trip, I reviewed the city planning website and learned all the zip codes and specific neighborhoods in midtown. I studied the area street by street. I did so much research that by the time I arrived, I already knew each neighborhood and the values of properties in them. As part of the course, we visited dozens of foreclosures each day. First we would walk the property to gauge how much the rehab would cost; then we would go inside and point out all the details of the interior. It was an amazing experience that taught me how to look at properties and how to value them.

After we returned from Kansas City, we had to write our first offers on properties. This was when I learned about hard-money loans. With this loan, you pay 3 to 5 percentage points of the loan amount up front plus a hefty interest rate, which was about 13 percent at that time. This was a high interest rate, but following my mother's advice about looking for opportunity amid danger, I thought the rate didn't matter as long as it moved me closer to the opportunity to make money. After I purchased the property, I could implement the strategy they taught us: BRRR—buy, rehab, rent, and refinance.

I found a foreclosure property in Kansas City that was $32,000 with an after repaired value (ARV) of $65,000. I found a hard-money lender who offered 65 percent loan to value (LTV) with a 13 percent interest rate, 3 points origination, and six months no payment while interest got rolled into the principal. I then got $10,000 financed by the same lender for renovation costs, which I completed within three weeks. Finally I did a cash-out refinancing with a conventional lender and received $15,000 cash back since the value of the home had gone up to $85,000.

With 80 percent LTV, a conventional lender would lend me $68,000, and after I paid off my hard-money loan and miscellaneous fees, I was able to do a cash-out after my refinancing. Not only did I not put any money down, when I refinanced, I took the $15,000 cash-out to pay off my credit card debt. After the renovations, I rented the property out and started making about $100 a month in positive cash flow. By now, we were in the middle of the historic recession, the market was horrible, and interest rates were sky-high, but among these crises, I started my *true* real estate investment career.

Loan amount (incl. $10,000 remodeling budget) = $65,000 * 65% = $42,250

Loan origination fee = $1,267.50

Six months' interest = $2,746.25

Misc. cost = $6,000

Total cost = $52,263.75

Refinance loan amount = $85,000 x 80% = $68,000

Cash out = $15,736.25

EXPANDING YOUR COMFORT ZONE

Having grown up with my mother's example of finding opportunities amid crises, it was not surprising that my own business grew during the riskiest real estate disaster in recent American history. In September 2008, after buying my Dallas duplex and Kansas City building, I was still working as a loan officer. Despite the fact that I was good with numbers, working behind a computer all day didn't fit my personality. I thrived on being outside and looking at properties. My brother-in-law introduced me to an asset management company. When they asked me to help them sell some of the foreclosure properties, I immediately agreed. I was given ten listings within an hour.

I had bought a few properties by taking advantage of risky loan products, yet I had no experience selling a property. It frightened me because it was out of my comfort zone, but I welcomed the challenge. I had to learn fast because the ten listings needed to get onto the market within days. I knew I had a lot of learning and catching up to do. For starters, I was told that I would need to place For Sale signs on the properties within two weeks and provide brokers with pricing opinions for each property with my own explanations.

I had to quickly learn graphic design techniques to create my signs; then I had to find a sign company to expedite their printing. When I went to pick up my signs, they told me I needed T-shaped posts. Posts! I barely had any money and had charged the printing of the signs. The cost wasn't even the hardest part: I disassembled ten posts with metal stakes, plus ten signs, and stuffed them into my small sedan. Once I had my car crammed, I headed to the first property.

Since my parents always taught my sister and me that first impressions are important, I always dressed nicely, no matter what. I quickly learned that hammering posts into the ground wearing a dress and heels in the California sun was no easy feat. No matter how many times I tried, my signs leaned. Over and over again, I tried getting those signs in the ground, but they were always askew. I was drenched in sweat wrestling with a sign when I spotted one neighbor watching me. I thought, *Oh, God. Pretend I'm fine. I'm fine.* I gave a quick wave and turned my attention back to my nemeses: the signs. In a fit of frustration, and having broken every fingernail, I called my husband and begged for help. He met me at the property and showed me how to use a rubber mallet to drive the stake in. He made it look easy, but even with the mallet, my signs were crooked. This was the biggest moment in my career to date, and all of my listings were advertised by crooked signs. It was almost like my first trademark. Who knew that the hardest part about teaching myself the real estate sales process would be those darn signs!

Once I got the signs up, I turned to the next obstacle: cleaning up the properties. Since these were foreclosures, some held evidence of squatters, like chicken bones and beer cans scattered about. Sometimes when I entered, the hair on the back of my neck would stand up, and I would get the feeling that I wasn't alone. I couldn't get the properties presentable due to holes in the wall, stolen copper plumbing, and missing toilets, but I could at least haul off the trash that was there. I also had to turn on utilities for each property and pay the bills with credit cards up front.

After getting the properties as presentable as I could and handling the utilities, I turned my attention to learning how to be a listing agent. As a listing agent for a foreclosure, you essentially become an asset manager as well. This means that you have to go back every week to inspect the property, take pictures, and send reports to the institution that owns it. Visiting ten properties weekly to create my reports and inspections proved to be time-consuming. Considering I was contending with LA traffic and properties spread over a seventy-mile radius, I spent a lot of time in the car hustling to sell these properties listed from $150,000 to as much as $650,000.

When selling a property, there are paperwork disclosures to prepare and contracts to draft. I had no experience with either, so I asked for help from friend who was a sales agent. She was nice enough to show me how to write up a contract. Then I hired a transaction coordinator to help me put together all of the paperwork. Despite needing to ask for help occasionally, I tried to do it all myself. I wanted to learn every detail of each step of the process.

Slowly, over the course of twelve months, the properties sold, and I was making more money than I had made before as an analyst. Despite how challenging and humbling the process was, I was enjoying it so much. I felt that I had found my purpose in life. Even during my struggles, I remember thinking of all the ways this process was going to change my life. I was willing to sacrifice hours of sleep and broken fingernails because I felt like this was it: this was my moment.

> **DESPITE HOW CHALLENGING AND HUMBLING THE PROCESS WAS, I WAS ENJOYING IT SO MUCH. I FELT THAT I HAD FOUND MY PURPOSE IN LIFE.**

I unknowingly began my real estate experience when I subleased my Santa Monica apartment and secured myself some monthly passive income. Feeling emboldened, I jumped into buying the Dallas, Texas, apartment that nearly sank me. I knew there were still opportunities ahead, so I talked John into purchasing a condo, which turned out to be rife with mistakes when it lost half of its value during the recession. This was a humbling experience that proved that I needed to learn more about the business to be successful. When I attended seminars, I learned from proven real estate investors. Though they were sometimes expensive, they turned out to be formative for my burgeoning career.

Despite selling ten foreclosure properties and having bought three properties, I knew I still had much to learn. I enrolled in postlicensing classes to improve myself. I was an astute student and finished the year-long Graduate Realtor Institute (GRI) designation in only three months. After that, I continued to learn and study and received more designations and certificates like e-PRO, ABR, SFR, and CDPE. The abbreviations started piling up after my name, and I started to gain confidence and credibility.

My mom was right all those years ago because my career was born during the worst possible time for real estate. It was a dangerous time to be involved in the market, especially for a beginner. I knew, however, from my mother's example, that if I was willing to be resourceful and creative, I could find opportunities that others weren't willing to seek. That's not to say it was all smooth from the beginning, but I had found my path, and I knew it. Now that I was on it, nothing would take me away.

ADVICE ON BUILDING A BUSINESS

Nobody wants to be poor forever. If you want to reclaim your finances and your future, listen to what experienced people are telling you and then do it. Everyone dreams, but not everyone takes action. Many people tell me they try to time the market right, but why wait? There are always opportunities; you just have to research, study, and discover them. No matter the crisis or the danger, seek out opportunity.

Sitting in front of these boxes where my parents used to worked til late in the night for their import and export business.

This was all the furniture I had when I moved into the West LA studio.

104

I was the first one being interviewed at the US Embassy because of my nicely organized complete documentations.

My mom's first time in Las Vegas where she was amazed by everything she saw.

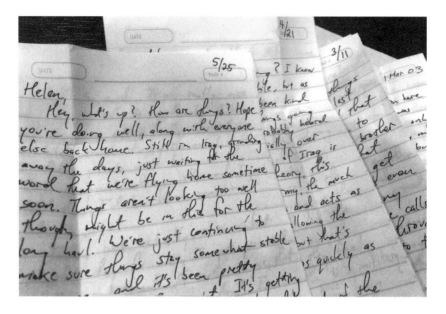

The letters John wrote to me during his first deployment.

On March 1, 2008, we had our beautiful ceremony after being married on paper for three years.

I would lay in bed thinking about how I was being held back by pregnancies while John's career took off full speed with his master's degree training, his burgeoning career, and his Fortune *magazine cover.*

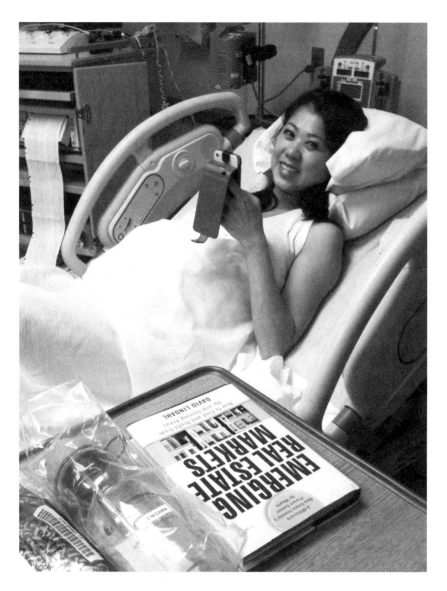

I continued to communicate with my clients and read real-estate-related books during my active labor for pain management.

No matter whether it's your first, second, or third child, it is exhausting, and it is difficult to maintain positivity especially when you are suffering from any kind of postpartum depression.

It's absolutely a blessing to earn the "America's Best" Award with my childhood friend, Susanna Leung, and the rest of the HAYLEN Team while raising our families.

109

It became my passion to share my stories with the opportunity given through the ForbesSpeakers platform.

All the obstacles and hardships brought me to find my HOME across the globe where I married an amazing man. Together, we raise our three amazing children and give them a forever-HOME memory to carry through the rest of their lives.

CHAPTER NINE

SACRIFICES BETWEEN FAMILY AND CAREER

J ohn and I knew we wanted to have a big family, though my plan (because I always had one) was to build my career first and my family second. It was 2009, and despite the deep recession, I had bought my first two rental investments—the Dallas duplex and the Kansas City home—and a primary home. I was also slowly selling off the ten properties I'd listed. While I waited for the remaining ones to sell, I continued to field calls, pursued more investment properties, and attended as many classes and seminars as possible.

One night, John and I were talking when he blurted out, "I think we're ready to have kids. Don't you think so?" I froze. This was the moment I'd been looking forward to. But I wasn't feeling happy; instead, I felt terrified. I remember thinking, *Everything will have to stop. My career is going to be over. What am I going to do?* I had just gained some confidence in my real estate career. Even though I wasn't making a lot of money, I was working toward something important. The only response I could muster was, "Oh my." My hesitation was obvious and confused John, "Wait a minute. You always wanted a family, right?" I replied, "I don't know if I'm ready" and ran to the bedroom.

Once alone, I realized I didn't feel the time was right to have a baby. Despite some success in my real estate ventures, I was still keenly aware that John and I were in financial crisis with our condo. In 2009, there were countless short sales and foreclosures happening across the country. I wasn't sure what our financial future held. I thought back to what my mother always said about finding opportunity in crisis. Did the same principle apply to family planning? Was there ever a good time to start a family? I decided to approach the growth of my family with the same bravado I had the birth of my business. The next day I told John that I wouldn't ever feel fully ready to start a family, but I knew that if we didn't start now, we would regret it as we continued to grow older. I would face any challenge the way I always do: head on. Let's just do it.

Not long after, I found out I was pregnant. I surprised John with the news, and we were elated. All my hesitations were replaced by joyful expectations. All of my focus went to the pregnancy and the future of the baby. My pregnancy hit me much harder than we expected. Seven weeks in, I started getting extreme bouts of vertigo. The episodes hit me so hard that I felt like I had lost control of my body. I threw up every day. I could not eat anything. After two weeks of unrelenting nausea, I had already lost ten pounds. Seeing how severe my condition was, John force-fed me protein shakes, much like my mom had done years ago in Hong Kong. I had no energy and eventually ended up in the hospital. The nurses had to give me two bags of intravenous fluids before I regained some energy.

By this time, John had left the military and was working for a defense contractor as a financial analyst. He was also going to school for his MBA. Both were over forty-five miles away from our home, and his commute took over an hour and a half of LA traffic each way. This was not going to work, as I needed lots of help. John and I agreed we should move closer to his family so we could have more help while he worked and attended school. By this time, the market was in a deep recession that showed no signs of ending. Our property value plummeted, so it made financial sense to do a short sale. Even though we could continue to pay—and we wanted to continue to pay so as not to damage our credit—the bank told us we had to default on our mortgage payments to be considered for a short sale. It was hard to feel like we were forced to become irresponsible homeowners. Because there were so many foreclosures and short sales happening, the banks were overwhelmed, and their short sale and foreclosure departments didn't communicate effectively. We had to let go of the property, and it stung. We put 5 percent down plus the cost of remodeling, so relatively speaking, it wasn't a large investment, but I was still ashamed. My goal had been setting us free through real estate, and I had been working so hard, and now it felt like I had failed myself and John. He gave me a wonderful reminder during this time, though, that letting the house go was a business decision that allowed us to move forward with our lives. It wouldn't make sense to hang on any longer.

We moved to a rental home on the west side to be closer to John's work and family. I was too embarrassed to tell anyone that we had lost our home. At the time, it felt like the appropriate strategic decision because we couldn't hold onto something that was losing value, plus, with the baby coming, it was too much to handle. Despite all of the impending change happening, we settled into our new rental and started preparing for the baby.

STUCK ON THE SIDELINES

While I was barely functioning, John got a call from *Fortune* magazine asking if they could interview him for a story they were doing about military personnel who had transitioned into the corporate world after being in the wars. They told him they wanted to fly him to New York for a photo shoot. I was so happy for him, but I will also admit that I was jealous. As I hung my dizzy head in a bucket, it felt like my life was changing for the worse while his was changing for the better.

I was too frail and weak to accompany John, so while he was in New York, his brother came by to check on me. When John returned, he said the magazine had decided to put his photo on the cover. The *cover*? Two life-changing moments happened concurrently: something bad for me and something good for John. I would lay in bed thinking about John's master's degree training, his burgeoning career, his magazine cover. My friends would call from all over the world to tell me they saw my husband in a globally known magazine. "You must be so proud," they crooned. It seemed like his career was taking off full speed while I was held back by this pregnancy.

Even though I could barely get out of bed those days, I still had to work. I wasn't willing to give up the momentum I had started. I didn't have assistants or anyone to help me out, so most days I lay in the bed gagging and typing with one finger. About six months into the pregnancy, the vomiting remained, but the nausea subsided a bit.

Suddenly the room didn't seem like it was spinning, and I was able to get a little more work completed.

Once I started feeling better, I realized I had been projecting so much negativity onto John. I felt like I had sacrificed everything—my health, my body, my career—but if I was being objective, he had sacrificed a lot too. It wasn't easy to work all day, go to school, and take care of a sick partner. I knew I was giving up a lot, and I didn't want to be consumed by resentment, so I started making an effort to see—really see—all that John was giving up as well. While most of his friends enjoyed MBA networking events, he had to come home and check on me instead. It was stressful for him to watch me feel so miserable. In reframing my thoughts, I was better able

> **IN REFRAMING MY THOUGHTS, I WAS BETTER ABLE TO APPRECIATE MY PARTNER AND BE LESS CONSUMED BY NEGATIVITY AND RESENTMENT.**

to appreciate my partner and be less consumed by negativity and resentment. Hopefully, this mindset would stay with me in the coming weeks because the baby was almost here.

I went to the hospital on my induction date filled with excitement. I had made a video for my baby the day before to document what I was feeling and thinking in that moment. (Also, as an avid planner, I needed to make that video just in case something happened to me.) I wanted my baby to know me and the joy I felt about the impending experience. At the hospital, I refused pain medication. I wanted to feel the sensations and fully experience the moment. The nurses kept asking if I was sure about the pain medicine. "If we wait too long," they warned, "you may not be able to have it when you want it." Obviously, the contractions hurt, but I smiled each time one passed. The whole labor experience was amazing, and

I was finally enjoying one aspect of the pregnancy. I successfully kept myself distracted from the pain by messaging with clients and thinking about work.

When my distraction method stopped working and the pain became too intense, I opted for an epidural. The birth was so beautiful. My mother stayed in the delivery room with me and John. When my baby was born, I was expecting the magical moment everyone told me about: "When you see your baby for the first time, you will fall in love instantly!" When they handed my son, Matthew, to me, I looked at him for the first time and thought, *Whoa, this baby looks weird. His nose is crooked; his ears aren't straight!* I was overcome with fear. Where was that feeling people told me about? I felt like I was holding a tiny stranger that had just arrived in my arms. My next thought stayed with me for the next two weeks: *Oh my God. I do not have the feeling of a loving mother!*

As I grappled with my own self-doubt, the doctors were pushing on my stomach to deliver the afterbirth and then stitching me up. My mother-in-law walked in, and there I was, exposed to the world, and I couldn't do anything about it. That beautiful feeling I felt during the labor and delivery was replaced with shame, guilt, and vulnerability. The nurses explained I had perineal tears during delivery and would need to wear diapers with ice packs in them for the next two weeks. What? No one ever told me about this part!

The following days were ugly. I couldn't walk. My breasts were engorged and painful. I would look down and see my shirt soaked with breast milk. Breasts were no longer sexy. My body was not sexy. It was just utilitarian and functional once I became a mother. The baby woke every hour crying, so there was never time or energy to focus on anything other than my new son's constant needs. I felt disgusted by the whole process. To be honest, I was mad at the world. I had such high expectations of this beautiful moment. Why didn't anyone tell me about the ugly side of mothering? I felt like I had been tricked.

My parents came from Asia to help out with the baby and take care of me—the Chinese way. My mother devoutly followed the Chinese traditions that forbid a new mother from taking a shower or washing her hair for thirty days. I was only supposed to touch warm water, never cold, and eat a strict diet that involved lots of chicken, sesame oil, ginger, and ten eggs each day. I decided this was all ancient superstition, and I showered and washed my hair anyway. I drank cold water and washed my hands in it. My mom would yell at me each time, and this added to the already tense environment.

After nine months of not being able to eat during pregnancy, my appetite finally returned. I would drink bowls of milk as if I couldn't get enough. My mother insisted I warm them, which I did to appease her and avoid a fight. My main function as a human being was to feed my baby. Every two hours I was pumping and then feeding my son in between. I didn't realize that nursing would be so painful and all-encompassing. I couldn't get any sleep. I remember one afternoon when my son was about two weeks old; I woke to my mother standing next to me trying to latch the baby to my breast. "What are you doing?" I asked, alarmed. She said, "I've been knocking on the door. You didn't wake up. Matty has been crying and needs to eat." I remember feeling too exhausted to even sit up. I was overwhelmed with embarrassment, frustration, resentment, and regret.

I had heard about postpartum depression (PPD), but during those first two weeks of new motherhood, I was too tired to think about how that might affect me. When you're in a depressive state, you're often too close to it to even recognize what it is. I kept looking for a way to rewind my life because I regretted the decision to be a mother. My thoughts worried me—*Why did I do this? Why don't I feel love toward this baby? Why do I want to run away from all of this?* I had only been a mother for two weeks, and already I was convinced I was bad at it. I felt like my friends and society had duped me into believing this would be beautiful when in reality, it was horrible and ugly.

I knew that I shouldn't be feeling this way about my baby and the mothering experience, so I hid my feelings and cried alone often. As I read more parenting books, I realized that I was probably suffering from PPD. I knew that giving into these thoughts could bring me further down and wreak havoc on my family. I remembered that when I was depressed in college, I took control of my mindset and started to feel better. Could I do the same with motherhood? I accepted the need to tackle this challenge, and I went to a new mothers' support group. *I would never have thought I needed a support group.* After a few days, I started to feel more loving toward my baby because I was able to find mutual understanding from other new mothers. It was still hard, but the darkness lifted enough to let points of light in.

After a month and a half, my parents returned to Asia. It was time to learn how to balance my new responsibilities on my own. I needed to find a new normal by taking care of my baby and my career. After all, one of the reasons I chose real estate was to have a flexible schedule that afforded time at home with my children. For the first six months of mothering while working, it felt manageable and doable. My son slept a lot and was happy when he was awake as long as I was holding him. I made most of my calls with him quietly tucked in my arms. *I can do this: I really can have a family and a career.* According to my plan, I was going to have it all.

THE MYTH OF ENTREPREMOM

When my son was five months old, I enrolled in a real estate seminar. I was still breastfeeding, so I had to lug my pump everywhere I went, but otherwise, I felt like my old self again. During the seminar, I had to excuse myself often to pump. When I asked a male hotel worker for a quiet place to pump, he said they didn't have a place for this purpose, but I could pay for a hotel room to do so. *Are you kidding me?* Finally, I talked to a female employee who empathized and took me to an empty conference room. I sat in that room alone, pumping milk for my baby, and I couldn't escape reality

> **I SAT IN THAT ROOM ALONE, PUMPING MILK FOR MY BABY, AND I COULDN'T ESCAPE REALITY ANY LONGER: I WAS NOT MY OLD SELF. I WAS A NEW PERSON—A MOTHER.**

any longer: I was not my old self. I was a new person—a mother. There might be new fathers at this conference, I thought, but they were able to stay with the group. They still owned their bodies, their careers, their futures. I felt like my body, career, and future had been hijacked. I knew that I wanted the pride of taking care of my son *and* owning a flourishing business, but could I actually have both? Or would I have to give up one to have the other?

When I returned to the seminar, one of the speakers was taking the stage. She was a successful real estate investor and mother to a young child. She gave a great talk, and after she finished, I chased her down. When I caught up to her, I told her I had a newborn at home and was struggling to figure out the balance. I told her, "I'm realizing that maybe I cannot do both jobs. How do you do it?" Her response was simple: "Ask for help." I told her I didn't have the money to hire help. She replied, "That's a myth. You are right that being in real estate means you're able to work from home, but there's no way you can take care of the baby and work at the same time. You have to get help." She told me that she worked from her home office and stopped to have lunch with her baby each day. "If you don't hire somebody," she asked, "how are you going to make any money? You have a choice: do work that's worth ten dollars an hour or pay someone ten dollars an hour to help you take care of the baby while you spend that hour doing something that will earn more than that." Her theory was sound and made sense, but I wasn't sure that I could actually implement it.

When I returned from the conference, my quiet, agreeable baby had transformed into a squabbling, insistent one. Suddenly when I talked on the phone with clients, my son wanted to babble along. He didn't sleep as much, and he often screamed for no discernable reason. He had developed his seven-month milestone: separation anxiety. I panicked. I knew I couldn't work like this. A few more weeks of this, and I finally admitted to my husband that I was struggling. "I'm torn. I don't know what to do," I told him. I explained what the conference speaker had suggested. John was quiet for a moment and then replied, "Do you really think you need to?" I fired back, "Well, lucky you, you get to go to work and just leave all this for me! I have to work and take care of the child at the same time!" In all honesty, my resentment had been building for months about this, and it was finally exploding in anger. It was all so unfair. He was still moving up in his career, while I lagged behind with this baby slowing me down more each day. In hopes of mitigating any further resentment, and to give myself some semblance of my career, I made the decision to hire help.

I found a nanny and scheduled her to work for five hours twice a week. She came between my son's morning and afternoon naps, which allowed me eight full hours of work. When she was there, it was amazing. I was getting so much done. Soon I was asking her to come more frequently. The formula was working—I was paying her ten dollars an hour while I did work that exceeded that hourly value, so I wasn't losing money. This was the first time I had asked for help, and though I didn't get the pride of "doing it all," I was able to continue building my business and my family.

It was 2011, but I was able to do eight to ten deals a year despite the deep recession. This was the most business I had ever done. I now had clients to work with and was bringing in income; I felt like a success to be doing both. This might all work out after all.

Since John's *Fortune* magazine article, he had gotten good exposure and received a call from Apple for an interview. We were still living in our LA rental at the time. I was nervous about what would come from this interview, but John was optimistic. "Let's just see where this takes us," he said. I adamantly replied, "We're not moving!" I was just starting to feel like I had some traction in my business. I had help, things were moving along well, so I was not, under any circumstances, going to give up my career momentum again.

John went for the interview and ended up getting an attractive offer from Apple. I didn't know what to do, so in my typical style, I started analyzing. I looked at the living expenses between LA and Silicon Valley. Even with his salary increase, was it worth it for us to move there? I did not want to move to Silicon Valley. I was doing well in my career for the first time, and I could not leave that behind. After some thought, however, I knew this was John's moment. I had started my career from scratch before, and I could do it again. This all sounds selfless, but it wasn't entirely. I was supportive externally, but I was angry internally. I was resentful and regretful, and I bemoaned having to be the one to sacrifice my career again.

By this time, our son was nine months old. We were grappling with this tough decision about John's employment offer when we got another bit of news: I was pregnant. This certainly pushed us to make a decision about relocating, and with another baby on the way, we needed the salary increase. We decided John would move first to a temporary housing in Silicon Valley so he could get settled in to his new job, and my son and I would stay with my in-laws until we could find a good housing solution for all of us.

People always say that each pregnancy is different. I was hoping this would prove true. When I was about five weeks pregnant, however, I started feeling familiar sensations—dizziness, nausea, vertigo. This pregnancy proved to be even worse, because in addition to feeling awful, I had a baby and a career to take care of. With John in Silicon Valley and me staying with my in-laws, I felt lonely and trapped. My resentment grew as John lived a life that seemed to grow fuller each day, while mine shriveled until it barely resembled the one I once knew and loved.

After about a month of being separated geographically, my son and I joined John in Silicon Valley. Even though I was sick and had an almost-one-year-old, I had to find us a place to live. John had to take business trips for his new job, and I was suddenly home with a baby, constant vertigo, and no support system. My anger continued to snowball. I was not happy with the move, and I grew more unhappy each day. I wondered where my life was taking me.

I spoke with friends during this time who told me to take a few years off from my career: "What's the big deal? When the kids are older, you can start again." This was not an option for me. I felt like no one understood. John was trying to be supportive and suggested that I could stay home without working. But I couldn't put my career on hold for two years because I would lose the momentum and clientele I had been meticulously building for years. I was already taking a large hit to my business by getting pregnant and relocating. So far, I had managed to keep my LA clients by hiring agents to show properties in my absence. Even though I was continuing to work for these clients, take their calls, and consult with them, I had to pay someone else to show properties. It was already a complicated feat.

I knew I had to go along with the plan I agreed to. After all, the baby would come, whether we had a home ready or not. After visiting more than twenty properties with my baby and growing belly in tow, I found a suitable rental home. We settled in, and I set up my office in a corner of the kitchen. I figured that would be the most efficient location because I could work and cook at the same time.

ACCEPTANCE AND PARTNERSHIP

My second pregnancy was just as difficult as the first. When it was time to deliver, I had a more realistic view of the ugliness that would follow. I had another amazing delivery, and my second son, Nathaniel, was born. Even though I was logically prepared for those familiar dark feelings, they hit me with full force anyway. This time, my PPD was even worse. With all my snowballing resentment in the previous months, I was ready to explode. This time, I wished for an antidepressant medicine that could change me and how I felt. I was lucky not to have thoughts about harming myself or others, but I loathed my husband. I felt that he was merely my housemate who occasionally helped with childcare. I was sad in a way that precluded passion or love.

My parents came to help me again with the second baby. This took some pressure off me, but my new reality allowed me even less freedom. I couldn't leave the house without lugging car seats and overstuffed diaper bags with me. I could never just take off and go. It literally took me two hours of preparation to leave the house. My second child was a lot more difficult than my first one. For a solid ten months, he woke every two hours. There were many nights that my husband and I would have to wake more than ten times in a night.

Even though I knew what to prepare for, after my second child was born, I was still overtaken by anxieties and resentments. I could only focus on what they had taken from me—my freedom, my passion, my marriage, my career. I missed the feelings of love and motivation I once had.

I started contacting other moms who were in similar situations. I asked one friend with a PhD and three kids under the age of three how she did it. She responded, "It's unfair, but I just accept it. It's hard, but it's love." I wanted to be more like that. I asked another professional mom with four kids how she managed without getting depressed. She said, "I accepted that this is my life as a mom." There was that word again—*acceptance*. I realized that I wasn't a damaged or broken mother and wife; I just hadn't *accepted* the new realities of my life. It wouldn't be my life forever, but it was my life at that moment. Could I accept it?

It took a while for me to learn acceptance. I could either complain, or I could surrender to what was and figure out how to make it better. I could become bitter, or I could accept that gender roles in parenting are not fair. I could get jealous, or I could see that my husband's career advancement wasn't just good for him, but it also was good for our family. Once again, changing my mindset helped me get out of a dark place. After that, I started to feel happier.

I looked forward to our lives. My husband felt more like my husband instead of a housemate. When I accepted the innate unfairness of parenting, I gave myself space to notice how hard he worked for our family. I noticed all the small ways he tried to ease my burdens. Rather than his shortcomings, I saw the beauty in his efforts. I had moments when I felt like the mother and wife I always aspired to be.

It's hard to separate the birth of my business from the birth of my children because the stories and events are all interwoven. It seemed the busier I got with work and children, the more disciplined I had to become about my mindset; the more I controlled my mindset, the more career opportunities I was able to handle. I actually ended up growing my business with each child's birth because I knew I had more chaos happening, and I had to leverage my time and mental energy effectively.

Once I was feeling better, and my second child was ten months old, I started thinking about a third child. I knew it would be rough, but I was determined to move on with our family plan. Soon, I found out I was pregnant again. I hoped this pregnancy would be different. Within a month of getting pregnant, however, I started feeling weak and nauseous. I returned to my familiar position in bed with a bucket within arm's reach. This pregnancy was so much harder because I had two children and a growing business. I would meet clients and immediately find the nearest place to throw up. As hard as it was for me, it was just as hard for my husband. He had to take the kids to work with him sometimes, drop them at school, pick them up, entertain them, and cook meals for all of us. In between, he was caring for me, and I had a new appreciation for all he sacrificed for us. He wasn't carrying the child, but he was carrying the burden. We were in partnership to share the burden in order to build a family together.

ADVICE ON BALANCING IT ALL

Many people envy working parents who have built businesses and families concurrently, but those people don't know the reasons *why* some parents fight so hard for personal and professional recognition. Those reasons are often rooted in insecurity or fear that children will feel their parents chose their careers over them. It's not easy being a parent, whether you are working or not. The greatest thing we can do in support of ourselves and others is to show the realities of parenting— it's beautiful some of the time and ugly most of the time. When we add more pressure on ourselves to portray beauty and competence, then we are setting ourselves up for resentment and bitterness. Social media makes parenting seem so easy and shiny. It's a lie. It's not always beautiful; in fact, it often isn't, especially in the early years. Be kind to yourself and honest about your struggles. Sometimes the greatest sign of strength is asking for help.

CHAPTER TEN

INVESTING IN REAL ESTATE

cannot remember a time when I did not have ambitions, both personal and professional. Occasionally being goal-oriented ended in disappointment, but more often than not, this drive served me well and provided me with short-term achievements that resulted in long-term successes.

After attending many real estate investment conferences, I was eager to use the strategies I'd learned to further secure my place in the real estate industry. I decided I was ready to flip my first property. Instead of relying on others in the field to send properties to me, I began actively seeking them myself. Since it was 2009 and there were many homes in foreclosure status, I often scoured government and bank websites. Thanks to my mentorship opportunity with Robert Allen's institute, I had already done extensive research studies on particular neighborhoods in Kansas City—street by street, zip code by zip code. I knew which areas were stabilized and which ones were trending in that direction. Since I didn't have a lot of money, I decided to focus on rougher areas of Kansas City.

I found one large property that interested me. I was able to view it in person and fell in love with its woodwork and unique features. From the beginning, I had a clear vision of the property's potential. I approached my mother-in-law and my mother about participating with me, and they both agreed to invest in this project so I could buy the property for $35,000. Our estimated rehab cost was $50,000 and after repair value (ARV) was $160,000. Since we didn't need to pay all $50,000 up front, I decided to use the credit card checks I received in the mail, which I'd been collecting in case of emergency. I hired a contractor, but she dragged out the timelines and kept changing her proposals. I fired her team to avoid wasting more time, and I made sure she signed a waiver of mechanic liens before I paid her the remaining balance. My goal at this point—because I always had one—was to build a trusted team of contractors and service teams in Kansas City, so I could rely on them for future projects. I knew this would be difficult in the beginning but would be an integral component of my future investing success.

Being that I was an Asian woman in my late twenties who looked even younger and lived many states away, I often dealt with vendors who didn't take me seriously. This wasn't a new challenge for me; it was one I had dealt with my entire life. The second contractor I hired was young and eager to work. We seemed to get along well at first. As we became more comfortable with each other, however, he called me a drama queen when I asked for updates and questioned his approach. I could tell he didn't take me seriously; after all, I wasn't the typical investor. I wondered if he would talk to me in the same manner if I were a man.

I spoke with my husband about the situation and asked if he would speak with the contractor. I listened to their phone conversation and was shocked at how respectful and polite the contractor was to my husband. I was upset by the realization that I would not be taken seriously in this industry. I had worked so hard. *This is mine,* I thought, *I earned it.* I felt like I had spent my whole life trying to prove myself to people, and here I was trying to prove myself to someone I employed! I decided this would not be a barrier to my investment career, so I viewed this as a challenge to slay the industry, no matter my age or gender.

It took about four months to finish the renovation project on this Kansas City property. By the time it was ready to hit the market, I was pregnant with my first child. The pressure was mounting to have this project sold as soon as possible. I spoke with real estate agents who gave me varying property value estimates ranging from $125,000 to $200,000. In this situation, many people would choose the agent with the highest asking price. I was more interested in an agent with strong marketing strategies who I could trust. I found an agent I liked, and we eventually sold the property after six months—my first real estate flip.

KANSAS CITY FLIP

Bought the property for	$35,000
Repairs and renovations	$60,000
Misc. costs	$2,000
Total amount in property	$97,000
Sold it for	$160,000
Profit	$63,000

When we closed the sale of this property, John and I called our respective mothers and told them we were paying back their original investment plus 50 percent return. It was an amazing feeling. My mother-in-law said, "When can we do this again?" Since my mother was an entrepreneur, she was particularly intrigued and wanted to know how I'd done it. I felt proud to share my gains with my family, and I was hopeful I could maintain this trajectory. By this point, I was about to have my first child, so it felt good to have some money in the bank and some investment experience under my belt.

FINDING NEW REAL ESTATE OPPORTUNITIES

After the birth of my first child, I could no longer travel to Kansas City or handle more rehab projects, but I wanted my earnings to continue working for me. So instead of pursuing real estate opportunities, I invested in trust deed notes, which earned me 11.5 percent annual interest, secured by collateral—real estate. Trust deed note investments meant I didn't need to visit properties, deal with contractors or vendors, or worry about rehab projects. I never lent more than 65 percent loan to value, so I was protected by the equity of the property in case the borrower defaulted. Essentially, I became a hard-money lender, allowing investors to buy rehab projects. I found a private money broker who sent me deals to review. I'd run my own research in my kitchen office, and if I agreed with the values, opportunities, and strategies, I would sign off and send my money. From there, I'd receive monthly interest payment checks.

When I was pregnant with my second child, and having moved to a new city, I spent a lot of time rebuilding my real estate sales business. I knew that I needed a contingency plan in case my business didn't work out. I needed more passive income. As I always did in periods of chaos and uncertainty, I turned to list-making and goal-generating. I typed out a list of goals, included how much money I wanted to make and how much passive income I wanted to generate over the next three, five, and ten years. I started with a one-year goal of making $3,000 per month of passive income; by year three, a $5,000-per-month goal; by year five, a $10,000-per-month goal; and by year ten, a $100,000-per-month goal. These numbers seemed too large and far-fetched, so I knew I was on the right track. You need to aim high to land close to it!

After my goal-making, I spent numerous hours in front of the computer figuring out ways to achieve these goals. I stayed up late at night poring over investment opportunities. I was looking for more single-family properties, but with each one I considered, I realized if my tenant moved out, I would have 100 percent loss of rental income on that property. It started to make less sense to me. I had learned about apartment investing in one of the seminars, but it had always felt too lofty. As I reconsidered my annual goals in front of me, I decided that if I wanted to earn big, I was going to have to play big.

I had already learned that you value apartments based on how you can control the net operating income. In other words, if I bought a property and increased its income, its value increased.

Value = Net Operating Income (NOI) / Cap Rate

NOI: I could increase the NOI by raising income—like raising rents—or by decreasing operating expenses—like changing all lights into LED bulbs or controlling the water usage. If I bought a ten-unit apartment building, for example, if I increased NOI by $100 per unit, this would result in a $1,000-a-month increase in gross rental income. Just with this one small change, I could increase the income per year on this property by $12,000. Now, if you know the market cap rate (which I'll explain in chapter 12) for your property in your area, then you can calculate the value increase. Using this same example, if my ten-unit property is in a neighborhood with a 10 percent cap rate, and I increase rent by $100 per month on each unit, then I increase my property value by $120,000. There was no way I could yield the same numbers by renting out single-family homes.

I became fascinated by this valuation method strategy, and I was confident I could make it work for me. It was scary to think about going from single-family homes to buying apartment buildings, but I knew high risks yield high rewards. This was also during the financial crisis, so I knew that my mother would urge me to look for opportunities. I was about six months pregnant with my second child by this time, so I knew that if I wanted to meet my projected goals, I was going to have to act fast.

I was still centering my search on the Kansas City area because I had done so much prior research there. I studied the city's twenty-year improvement plans and looked at the emerging areas of the market. I knew if I could find a property in an emerging market, it had the potential to stabilize and become a stronger market. I found a twelve-unit property that seemed promising. Even though I didn't have $465,000 for the asking price, I called the seller to get more information. He explained that he was selling the property because he ran out of money for repairs. It was a twelve-unit property, but only four units were occupied. My head was spinning with all of the creative ways I could get involved without spending a lot of money. He said he would need roughly $60,000 for repairs. I asked him if I could help him with repairs for a partial ownership. I didn't really know how I was going to do this, but I figured I could sort out the financials later. He said it sounded like a great idea and that he would think about it.

In the meantime, I analyzed how much cash flow I could get from the property and how much investment I'd be contributing. I knew I could use the BRRR strategy (mentioned in chapter 8)—buy, rehab, rent, refinance. If I could buy it with cash or hard money, then I could repair, refinance, and rent it out. If it all worked out, it would be a great source of cash flow, and the property would continue to increase in value.

The reality was that I wasn't in the position to buy the apartment, but I kept analyzing it and researching it nonetheless. During one conversation, the owner said, "I'm desperate to get out of this. I think I'm just going to have to short sell." I knew this meant that I would then be working with a bank instead of the seller himself. I knew how a short sale worked, so I asked if we could start by dropping the asking price from $465,000 to $225,000, which changed my strategy entirely and left me a chance at landing the property.

I immediately started working on an offering memorandum to solicit for investors to act as private money lenders. I was willing to offer an 8 to 10 percent preferred interest rate, and the investor could then use this property as collateral. They would lend me 80 percent of the value, and I would come up with the remainder. In my presentation, I included my research on the area, nearby amenities, financial analysis, market research, and most importantly, my contingency plans as well as different exit strategies. I was proud of my presentation. There was just one problem: I was too scared to share it with anyone. I paused.

One day, I called the apartment owner again, and he said he had just accepted another offer.

When I got off the phone, I fell onto the floor and cried so hard I started hyperventilating. I was over eight months pregnant with my second child by this time. I called my husband and told him what had happened. He tried to calm me and reminded me it was OK if we didn't own the apartment. But in my mind, this building was to be our family's contingency plan. It was so damn hard to raise one baby while I worked, not to mention multiple children. In addition, it seemed impossible to rebuild my real estate brokerage business in this new city with two babies under one and a half years old. I knew I needed some passive income to feel secure and independent from my husband. His response was that if my business didn't work out, we'd live frugally. I said, "No, I've lived like that my entire life. I'm done. I want to feel financial freedom!" I wailed, "I have less than six weeks before the baby is born! I need this. I cannot start this process all over again; I don't have time. This was supposed to be *it!*" My crying caused intense contractions while I was on the floor. I scrambled around the kitchen to find a paper bag to breathe into, to not cause any harm to my baby. I vowed to always remember this lesson: never lose a deal because of inaction.

I VOWED TO ALWAYS REMEMBER THIS LESSON: NEVER LOSE A DEAL BECAUSE OF INACTION.

The next several weeks were rough. I felt like nothing was working out. My second baby, Nathan, was due in a month, and I missed my goal of securing passive income before the birth. I continued to follow up with the seller, in hopes that the deal would fall through. Three weeks after I'd lost the deal, I received a call from the seller. He explained that the other buyer was backing out. This was it. This was my ticket. "I'll make an offer! I'll buy it!" I declared. I asked how much the other offer was, and he said $150,000. I couldn't believe the price had dropped so significantly. I quickly submitted my letter of intent to buy the property for $125,000. I did not have any proof of funds, but I sent out the offering memorandum I had prepared previously to my network of past clients and investors to solicit a private money lender. I received a few notifications of interest, and within two days, I had secured an investor and provided proof of funds. The offer was accepted!

I immediately started planning for our due diligence process. It was two weeks before giving birth to my second child, and I went into overdrive getting things coordinated. I scheduled several inspections, appraisals, and interviews with property managers and contractors. Because I was so pregnant and unable to travel, I sent my husband and his brother Peter, who had been working in the real estate corporate world, to Kansas City. The investor also wanted to see the property and the area before the deal was complete, so he accompanied them. I had the entire itinerary set up, and all they needed to do was to show up at the appropriate times and ask the questions I had provided. Even though I had delivered copious research to my investor, he was shocked by the area. There were boarded houses and rough neighborhoods. He saw what was in front of him, not its potential.

I knew from calling the city planning department that the street was part of a ten-year improvement plan. I knew this was a high-risk and high-reward property. If I could manage the property well in the next decade, I would potentially yield even higher rewards upon the completion of the revitalization plan. The investor didn't share this vision, however, and when they returned from the trip, he said rather than lending the money, he wanted to go in 50 percent on the deal; furthermore, he wanted to recapture his investment before I could take any profits. After more negotiating, during which I was unwilling to give up 50 percent of the deal, he ultimately backed out. In a way, I was relieved because I didn't want to give up 50 percent of my equity, and I didn't want to give up my initial profits.

However, here I was with a great property, but I only had about $20,000 to put toward it. My mother-in-law was still pleased with her profit from our previous single-family-home rehab and offered to invest $50,000 in the project. At this point, my parents arrived to help me prepare for my second baby's arrival. As I told my mom all about the property, she got excited. In those moments, it was easy to see from whom I got my entrepreneurial spirit. Though my mother couldn't contribute any money at that time, she encouraged me to be resourceful and find a way. She sat with me in my kitchen office brainstorming ways to come up with the remaining $55,000. "I'm so close this time, Mom. I need to make this work, but where do I get this money?" At that moment, I looked at the shredder in the corner stuffed with junk mail ready to be shredded by the end of the week. "Oh my God! This is it!" I said. I pulled several credit card checks out of the trash that were ready to be shredded. I had previously called all of my credit card companies to increase my credit lines. I spread them out on the table and realized I had at least $30,000 in available credit in my trash can. On top of that, the credit card checks offered zero interest for fifteen months. I looked at the checks; then I looked at my mom. "Did I just find money in my trash can?"

I LOOKED AT THE CHECKS; THEN I LOOKED AT MY MOM. "DID I JUST FIND MONEY IN MY TRASH CAN?"

I started jumping up and down—not an easy feat at nine months pregnant. "This is it!" I screamed. I knew that I could pull money from my credit cards, and within the fifteen months of zero interest, I could rehab and refinance to pay the credit cards off. I was still approximately $20,000 short, so I needed to lower the purchase price. I pulled out the inspection reports and combed through them. There were quite a few necessary repairs. I called the lender and started negotiating, requesting a price reduction to $100,000. I knew this was a ridiculously low offer, but all I could do was try and allow them to counter back. Several days later, the lender wrote back and agreed to my reduced offer—$100,000! I immediately wrote $30,000 worth of checks from my credit cards to myself. One week later, I gave birth to my second child. A few days after that, I closed on my first apartment complex.

INVESTING IN OUR OWN HOME

Life only got more complicated after this. With two young children and burgeoning real estate investment and brokerage businesses, I was emboldened to achieve financial security—if not for me, then for my growing family. I soon learned that I was pregnant with a third child. With a one-year-old, two-and-a-half-year-old, and one on the way, I started thinking about another investment: our forever home. Before the birth of each of my first two children, we had moved. It seemed the third would be no different because our rent had increased 10 percent. It was 2013, the market was recovering, and the bidding wars were fierce. I wanted to buy a home, but I was too nervous after the foreclosure to take the chance. I dragged my husband to house after house. There was one house that we both liked, but I was hesitant because I had already researched the property and knew the owner had recently bought it and was flipping it. I thought, *If I buy this house, somebody else is going to make a ton of money. I should be the one making money instead of the one spending money.* My husband wasn't any closer to a definite opinion than I was. "Talk to me like a client," he said, in an attempt to get my objective advice rather than my subjective emotion. "OK," I said, "Does this house have everything on your checklist?" He responded jokingly, "I only want two things: a window in every bathroom and a wine fridge." I said, "You're the easiest client ever." He used the same exercise on me, and I realized the house had many of my must-haves—one-story, open floor plan, plenty of rooms, large yard for the kids to play, extra space for future expansion, detached garage, and a semicircular driveway. I realized this house had everything I desired, so why was I so hesitant? I could advise my clients rationally, with no emotion involved; with my own home, however, my fear of making a mistake overrode all my rationale.

For the three years after we lost our first condo, I avoided buying a home for ourselves because it wouldn't generate any income. I wanted to buy investment properties that increased my return. I didn't want the hassle of maintaining a property, and the market also had gone up for three years by this time, so I was afraid of buying at the top of the market. I knew I would have told my clients to take the leap and seize the low interest rate, tax benefits, and housing stability. But I continued having trouble being objective. I returned to my familiar strategy for figuring out next steps—analysis. I analyzed schools to see their trends in scoring, and I analyzed the property values of several areas. At the end, I knew that if we purchased a home, we would be there for at least ten years. The home would certainly appreciate in that amount of time. Also, with the mortgage interest and property tax write-offs, our monthly payment actually would end up being very close to the rent we were paying. We could actually budget our housing expenses for thirty years rather than wondering how much our landlord might increase rent next year, or if they might sell the place.

Despite the seller receiving multiple offers, we ended up getting the house we wanted. We were no longer at the mercy of a landlord. There were costs of homeownership, but the appreciation of the property was far more than we would spend. It didn't matter if the market was up or down, because we knew we would stay here for at least ten years, so we would certainly build equity.

Just a short time after we moved into our new home, our third child was born—a girl. I felt such pride bringing her *home*. A forever home. Within three and a half years, we had a family of five and a beautiful, permanent home that our children would build memories in. I love knowing that when my children are grown, they will always remember the hallways they ran, the yard they explored, and the security they felt within these walls. This is not just a house; it is a foundation that my husband and I have laid for our children.

We had built so much equity since purchasing our permanent home, and we were able to secure a home equity line of credit (HELOC) for more investments. Instead of using the HELOC to buy a depreciating asset like a car or a boat, we used the money to remodel our apartment buildings to increase their value. This became a strategy I would come to rely on: using home equity to invest in appreciating assets. The increase in income on the investment property covered our monthly payment on our HELOC. In this way, the purchase of our primary home was a smart investment in our personal and financial future.

There are values of homeownership that don't show up on any spreadsheet. I learned at a young age how fulfilling and satisfying stability can be, and I also know how disorienting it can feel when that is ripped away from you. After we bought our home, I felt calmer and more peaceful than I had in a long time. Our lives flourished even more because of the constancy we enjoyed. The calmness and stability I have felt has cemented my opinion of homeownership forever. My whole life has been in pursuit of the next step, the next goal, the next achievement. Now I realize that all of my efforts have been in pursuit of one true purpose: home. Though this purchase differed from my other ones because it doesn't provide passive income, it is still one of my proudest acquisitions because it is an investment in my family's future. It gives me the same feeling I had as a six-year-old, feeling happy and proud of the home my parents bought for us. It's been almost forty years of seeking, and I've finally found what I was looking for. I'm finally home.

ADVICE ON RENTING VERSUS BUYING

You won't be able to get security from renting. In almost all cases, your monthly payment will go up annually. When you own a home, however, you know how much your payment is going to be for the next thirty years, assuming you don't refinance. You can take ownership of your home and take active measures to increase its value. You have complete control. If you improve and maintain your property, your home will appreciate. If you use your home equity wisely (see chapter 12), you can use your home to purchase other investment properties. Those stable markers help guarantee your future financial security.

CHAPTER ELEVEN

SUCCESSES

T here are challenges working in the real estate brokerage industry. Many brokerages told me that I could not combine both commercial and residential real estate businesses. They said, "You should only focus on one or the other." But with my firm objective of helping clients build their real estate portfolios, starting from their primary residence to apartment buildings and eventually commercial properties, I could not see how I could separate them. One day as I was showing a client some retail properties, a commercial real estate broker took a look at my business card and dismissively said, "I've never heard of you before." I'm sure he meant that he didn't recognize me, though I couldn't help but think that he also meant that he hadn't seen someone who looked like me in this role before. It's true that I didn't fit the stereotypical commercial real estate agent profile of a Caucasian male in his sixties. As a female Asian residential agent in my thirties, I definitely stood out.

I have earned numerous residential real estate designations. However, in order to prove my professionalism and expertise in commercial real estate, I started searching for a designation for commercial real estate. I found the designation of Certified Commercial Investment Member (CCIM)—a designation that focuses on education, leadership, and market excellence. It takes an average of three years to complete the courses, with recommendations, a satisfactory commercial real estate portfolio requirement, and a six-hour final exam. Only 6 percent of commercial real estate agents hold this designation, making it the most prestigious designation in the industry. I tried out the two-day introductory class, with its emphasis on analytics and spreadsheets, and needless to say, I was hooked.

I fell in love with the classes and was determined to get more involved and be seen among other commercial real estate agents. So I started attending local CCIM chapter meetings consistently, despite their being located over an hour away. The meetings were held at a private country club in a room filled with older Caucasian males. I did not fit in, and I found that there were always discussions using terms I wasn't familiar with. As uncomfortable as I felt, I continued to attend the meetings regularly.

Once I started showing up consistently, I began to have more conversations with everyone. I'd like to think they respected my persistence, but it might also have been their realization that I wasn't going anywhere. It was while I was still taking one of the CCIM classes that I found out I was pregnant with my third child. I felt the familiar clock ticking on how much time I could devote to my career before the bleary-eyed struggle of caring for a newborn began. Again.

CHANGING THE FACE OF THE INDUSTRY

Tim, a classmate from one of my CCIM classes who specializes in the industrial leasing business, had also started attending the monthly chapter meetings. One day after the meeting, he said he had an opportunity to submit a proposal for a one-hundred-unit multifamily affordable housing listing. "I have this opportunity, but I specialize in industrial leasing. I know you specialize in multifamily. Would you be interested in working together to create a proposal and see if we could get this listing?" It was an urgent request because the proposal was due in one week. Up until that point, I had never had a multifamily listing, much less an affordable housing one. I had bought or helped clients to buy multifamily properties, but I had never listed any—especially as large as one-hundred-units. This was a $12 million listing!

He was leveraging my experience in multifamily and my marketing skills from residential real estate, while I was leveraging his experience and skill in technical writing and his relationship with the seller. Our skill sets complemented each other very well, and we became great partners—and besides, working with a man would assuage any biases people held against me.

When an opportunity is presented, you cannot be indecisive. I learned this valuable lesson with my Kansas City apartment complex, where my indecisiveness almost cost me my future. I knew if I encountered obstacles, I'd figure them out, just as I always did. Even though I did not know anything about affordable housing, I studied intensely to ensure I was equipped with any knowledge I might need during our marketing process.

WHEN AN OPPORTUNITY IS PRESENTED, YOU CANNOT BE INDECISIVE.

This deal was an amazingly validating experience. I had only been in Silicon Valley for a couple of years, and now I was presenting a one-hundred-unit project to well-known, affluent developers. We received eight offers, and the offers went a million dollars over asking price. The ultimate reward for me was learning more about my own skills and strategies. I also learned that I could leverage my residential real estate marketing as an asset with commercial real estate transactions. Best of all, Tim and I continued to collaborate, and five years later, we had completed tens of millions of dollars' worth of transactions together.

After this deal, my reception at meetings changed. Suddenly I had clout, a reputation. I could see people acknowledging me and engaging in more conversation with me. Everyone looked at me and talked to me differently. I would never fit the typical commercial real estate image people held, but I could break down traditional barriers. Instead of changing who I was or taking on the Herculean task of changing the stereotype, I was arming myself with education. When I opened my mouth, it was clear I knew what I was talking about, and that was what mattered most.

With the newfound respect of my peers, I continued to attend CCIM chapter meetings every month until I gave birth to Elizabeth. Just two months after her birth, I started volunteering on varying committees. I helped expand the chapter down into Silicon Valley, partially for a selfish reason—to be closer to home. One year later, they asked me to be on the board. Another two years later, I was nominated to serve as secretary, then as treasurer, and eventually I became the president for NorCal CCIM in 2020—their very first female Asian immigrant president.

It took years and dedication to earn this recognition, and many people asked me how I changed the industry. I could have chosen to never go back to these meetings because I did not fit in. But I stayed, allowing the others in the community the opportunity to see and accept who I am. I'm not the typical agent, but why would I want to be? I have built a loving family, a successful career, and a breadth of knowledge, all while maintaining my authenticity. Here I am.

TWO FACES OF SUCCESS

There is an ancient moral code in Hong Kong that many women live by—入得廚房, 出得廳堂. "You can be in the kitchen; you can be out in social settings." It's an expression that encourages women to excel domestically and socially. When I was eight years old, I wrote on my school paper about my dream for my future: becoming a woman who can 入得廚房, 出得廳堂. I wanted to be the type of woman who could keep a good house and shine brightly on my husband's arm in social situations. However, the older I got and the more responsibilities I shouldered, the more I realized this expression is difficult to live up to and can sometimes overburden women with its expectations.

There is certainly the myth of the superwoman who can work all day, juggle the kids, make dinner at night, and be grateful and accommodating each day. Are there truly such women? Now that I am a top producer in my area, hold leadership roles, sit on boards of directors, chair many task forces, and serve as president for a prestigious professional organization, in addition to writing a book and joining the ForbesSpeakers family, many women say to me, "How do you do it all?" But they don't see the pain—to get here and remain here. Despite these accolades, I still feel like a failure in many ways.

Each time I feel overwhelmed, it's easy to think my vulnerability is a weakness rather than a human attribute. When anyone rises to the top, no one sees the breakdowns in the middle. I'm here to proclaim that there were—and will continue to be—breakdowns on any rise. I want to be real about this because otherwise I do a disservice to all people trying to find the elusive balance. It's a tricky process, and it's fluid. You might find the balance one day and then lose it the next.

Much of my message for entrepreneurs is about finding balance through delegation. You cannot do it all, whether at home or at work. You need a partner in both realms. I once thought that a partnership meant my husband should be in the business with me. Looking back, I realize the way he could help me at work was to offer his support at home. That's how he could be a partner in my career—by championing it. I offer him the same, and now we're both excelling in our own careers while supporting each other.

You can't have it all, all of the time, but you can have it all some of the time. When I am at a leadership conference and my husband is at home caring for the children, I feel like I have it all. But the next week, when my husband is on a business trip, and I'm swamped by the details of domesticity, I feel like I have a deficit. The important thing to remember is that partnership requires sacrifices.

When I get overwhelmed, friends say I need to give up something. What am I supposed to give up? My husband said recently, "You do have a lot on your plate—volunteering, work, family, speaking. If you give up some volunteer work, will you be happier?" I said, "No, I enjoy volunteering; I feel like this is part of me." He went through and asked about each sphere of my life, and I repeated that I needed all of them to make me, *me*. He answered, "There's your answer then. Don't give up on the things that define you and that make you happy. If you do, you compromise some of your happiness." The key is not to give something up; it's to scale back. So I do this by delegating—hiring a part-time nanny, splitting my work with team members, sharing parenting responsibility with my husband, and so forth. You can have it all, but you cannot do it all if you do everything yourself.

Though my brokerage business has grown over the years, much of the struggle remains the same. I still get overwhelmed and overburdened. I still feel like I show a put-together face to the world and my family, and sometimes a harried one when I am alone. There are two faces of success, and oftentimes, neither one is pretty. But it is OK—they are authentic, and they're mine.

After so many years of struggle, I finally built my American Dream: I built a family with my supportive husband, and we made three beautiful children. I also built a growing and successful real estate sales business and became one of the top real estate agents in Silicon Valley. I gained some recognition within the industry by volunteering in different real estate organizations and have been nominated to different leadership roles. Eventually, I brought my parents to the United States to live with me. It was a monumental moment for me. Although I couldn't buy the Ferrari, as I had promised my father on the day I left Hong Kong, I am providing a much better life for my parents. It was not an easy decision for my parents to leave their network and the places they are familiar with. But my goal is to be able to care for them as they age.

In just short of a year after their move, my father had a heart attack and underwent a triple bypass and a valve replacement surgery. Aside from the countless doctor visits, I was restructuring my company, preparing to host a large forum that boasted many prominent speakers, including the city mayor, and attending CCIM Leadership conferences and ForbesSpeakers Forums on top of my real estate work. As I was rushing from appointment to appointment, I received a call from my sons' school saying one of them appeared to have pink eye. I would need to pick them both up, take them to the doctor, and possibly keep them home for the week. *That's it,* I thought. *I can't handle one more thing.*

I did what many people do in this digital age when they feel maxed out and ireful—I turned to social media. I posted to an online group of real estate moms about how stressed and overworked I was. How is it that I am in the top 1 percent of agents in my area and appeared to be able to handle so much, yet I felt so incompetent and distracted? I lamented the days when I could focus on one task and do it well. I asked, "Does anyone else feel this way?" I quickly received 175 comments. Apparently I wasn't alone.

> **THERE ARE TWO FACES OF SUCCESS: THE ONE PROJECTED OUTWARD, AND THE ONE VIEWED INWARD. WHEN I FEEL ADEPT IN MY CAREER, I FEEL INEPT AT HOME. WHEN I FEEL LIKE SUPERMOM AT HOME, I FEEL LIKE MY CAREER GETS SNUBBED.**

There are two faces of success: the one projected outward, and the one viewed inward. When I feel adept in my career, I feel inept at home. When I feel like supermom at home, I feel like my career gets snubbed. Despite how painful these imbalances can sometimes be, they are important and essential reminders of human vulnerabilities. In these moments, you can choose to continue falling, or you can stand up, brush off, and get back to the work at hand.

ADVICE ON THE TWO FACES OF SUCCESS

I once had a man with decades of experience in the commercial real estate business tell me, "Don't post glamorous headshots of yourself because you don't fit in when you do that." I said, "That's my face! That's who I am." That exchange always reminds me that I don't need to match anyone else's preconceptions. For years, I have heard that I am too young, too nice, or too feminine to succeed.

When I first moved to Silicon Valley and started my real estate brokerage business, no one knew who I was. When I arrived at showings or meetings, people would look at me side-eyed and ask what company I was with. I would answer, "I'm Helen Chong. I own my own company." They would mutter, "Oh, really? You look so young." This was incredibly frustrating, and I don't want to give the impression I always rose above it. It bothered me, but I never let it overtake me. The frustration was what motivated me to do better and break the molds in which they so desperately tried to fit me.

The reality is that no matter what you look like and no matter what field you are in, there are people who won't respect you on first sight. How do you win them over? By equipping yourself with knowledge. This is one reason education has been so powerful for me. My advice is to spend less time focusing on the unfairness and more time proving people wrong.

CHAPTER TWELVE

APARTMENT INVESTING ANALYSIS

U p to this point, I have shared my story—from my meager childhood in Hong Kong to my full adulthood in California. Though I have shown how my own mindset has affected my success and failures, now I want to share my proven strategies for investment. From my work with my clients over the years, I have learned that though many people are interested in real estate investing, they don't know how to start. There are too many options, too many players, too many strategies. In this chapter, I will share the practical advice that I have learned over my decades of investing so that you can start building your confidence and your wealth today.

GETTING STARTED

Though each buyer and circumstance is different, there are some general pieces of advice that I share with all of my clients. Though some of them might sound basic, they have become the foundation of my own real estate strategies.

THE FIRST SIX SIMPLE STEPS

1. **Understand your objective.** Too many people want to invest but don't understand what they are looking for. There are many strategies you can deploy in real estate investment, and it is important to understand your primary investment objective: quick cash, cash flow to replace income, building equity, or a combination of these. Knowing your goal will ensure that you find the right kind of property—with the right amount of risk—to suit your needs.

2. **Know your available cash.** Figure out how much cash you are able to gather for real estate investing purposes. Do you have a 401(k) plan that you can convert into a self-directed 401(k)? Stocks? A home equity line of credit (HELOC)? Credit lines?

   Understand your HELOC. Imagine you are twenty-five years old and used $60,000 as a down payment on a $300,000 home. Twenty years later, you have paid the mortgage down to $150,000. The property is now worth approximately $500,000 (your property's appreciation depends on its location). By the time you are forty-five years old, you've earned $350,000 worth of equity. You can apply for a HELOC up to 80 percent loan to value, which means the bank will allow you to have combined mortgages up to $400,000 ($150,000 first loan plus $250,000 HELOC). This creates a $250,000 credit line, similar to a credit card. You pay a monthly balance on the balance you used with only a nominal annual fee. One of the reasons so many people went into foreclosure or short sale in the 2008 recession is because they had pulled the equity out of their homes and bought depreciating assets (like cars and boats), and then the market tanked. If they had bought an investment property with positive cash flow, they could have supplemented their loss of income.

For example, if you have used $100,000 of the HELOC to invest, and if the interest rate is at 5 percent, that's $5,000 interest payments annually. Divide it by twelve months, and your monthly interest payment is only $416.67. You could use this $100,000 as 25 percent down payment on an investment property that's worth $400,000 and generates $2,000 monthly rental income, which will give you great positive cash flow.

3. **Know your loan options.** Now that you have a down payment, you need to know your loan options. There are banks for almost all types of borrowers.

   ▫ **National banks** typically have stricter guidelines but they have the best loan rates.

   ▫ **Mortgage brokers** can help you find banks that have looser guidelines (and may not require as much documentation), though their interest rates are often higher.

   ▫ **Hard-money lenders (HML):** Many people shy away from them because of the hefty loan fees, 1–3 percent

origination point, and 7–12 percent interest rate
options. Hard-money lenders typically lend 65–70
percent of the purchase price (or, in some cases, of
the after repaired value). They require interest-only
payments with a six-to-twenty-four-month loan term,
and they can fund your deal in less than fourteen days.
As long as you are still making a profit, this option is the
easiest way to get your foot into the real estate investing
world and not miss an opportunity.

▫ **Credit cards** are one of the methods I have used, but
this can be risky for an undisciplined person. As I
mentioned in a previous chapter, I called all of my credit
card companies and requested a credit line increase. I
spread my balance through numerous cards to ensure
the balances were under 40 percent of the credit limit
in order to maintain my good credit score. Credit card
companies sometimes send out credit card checks with
an introductory rate for twelve to fifteen months and 2
point transaction fee. It's a much cheaper option than
a hard-money lender. But you have to make sure you
have several good exit plans to pay it back in full within
the introductory time period.

▫ **Private funds:** Lastly, family members and friends may
have some savings or retirement funds that need to earn
a better return. You will need to prepare an offering
memorandum to earn their trust to invest in you. That
leads to the following steps.

4. **Perform market research and analysis.** One of the most common questions I'm asked is where to invest, and many people get stuck here. There is no one-size-fits-all answer, so you must conduct market research to identify areas with strong potential. For instance, there may be areas within a reasonable commute time from a metropolitan statistical area (MSA) that are considered emerging markets and on the upswing of the real estate cycle. You should also study your city's general planning to see if there are any revitalization programs in the works in certain neighborhood pockets.

Choose your markets: Most of my clients start off with a broad range of areas. To be an exceptional investor, you have to do extensive research. It is important to focus in just two or three cities, so you can tell whether a property is a good value immediately. There are a few factors you should consider when you conduct your market research, including population growth, job growth, median home value growth, crime trends, income trends, and local city planning. When I work with my clients, they start with ten or more randomly chosen cities and fill out their researched data in our two-step market analysis spreadsheet. We then select the top three best areas. Lastly, we study the general plan issued by the local planning department and pinpoint the exact neighborhoods we will focus on. The exercises are completely done by our clients, as you must consider your comfort level before selecting an area.

*You can download a copy of our spreadsheet by visiting our website: www.PowerToChangeLives.com.

---

5. **Plan your exit strategies.** It's important to have multiple exit strategies. If your intention is to rehab and flip, you should also be prepared to rent it out in case of a market change. Will the rental income provide you with a positive cash flow? If you are able to demonstrate to your potential partners that you have thought of different scenarios, they will have more confidence in investing with you.

6. **Build your team.** Your team includes a real estate consultant or agent, a property manager, inspectors, lenders, contractors, and potentially others. You need a strong team on the ground because you have to be able to delegate. It may take a few hires before you settle for the right team. A team can make or break you, as I shared with you in chapter 8. Always ask for referrals and check references. Beware of those people who can't be found anywhere online. Most trusted professionals rely on referrals and their reputation.

UNDERSTANDING THE DIFFERENCES BETWEEN RESIDENTIAL AND COMMERCIAL REAL ESTATE

VALUATION DIFFERENCES

To value a one-to-four-unit residential building, we will use the **Comparable Sales Approach**, which means property's value will fluctuate compared to the sales price your neighbors received from selling their property. However, we value five-plus-unit residential buildings by using the **Income Approach,** which means the property's value relies on the net operating income (NOI) the building is bringing in.

First, let's start by understanding this formula:

Cap Rate = Net Operating Income ÷ Value

Cap Rate: Every market has a cap rate as a benchmark. Here's a simple way to understand cap rate: it's the rate of return you can expect on the first year, assuming you are purchasing it with cash. You can have different cap rates depending on different areas, even within the same city. For example, in San Francisco, your cap rate can be as little as 2 to 3 percent if purchasing with cash in 2019. If you look at Kansas City, though, you can expect a 7 to 8 percent cap rate in the same time period, which will allow for some positive cash flow, even with a 5 percent mortgage rate financing. Just like anything else in life, the higher the risk, the higher the potential return. It may seem that it does not make sense to buy in such a low-cap-rate markets. I will show you later how you can earn tremendous values when you buy in a low-cap-rate market.

Net Operating Income (NOI): NOI is the most important number to know for your analysis, especially for multiunits, because it determines the sales price of the property. If you know how to play with the income or the operating expenses, you can drastically change your property value.

You may increase NOI by increasing rent rates, adding storage units to rent, renting out parking spots, adding laundry facilities, or charging tenants partial utilities. Conversely, you can decrease operating expenses by switching to LED lights, separating out utility meters, or lowering vendor costs.

Valuation Method: Properties with one to four units are considered residential properties and use the Sales Comparison method to provide a value. When your neighbor sells, for example, your property value will adjust accordingly. However, once a building has five or more residential units, we use an Income Approach valuation method. The valuation relies on the income the building can generate.

One reason I enjoy working with multifamily units is because it gives me a greater level of control on the valuation. As long as I can manage the property and control the NOI, I can increase my property value. As an example, I completed a repositioning project on a twelve-unit apartment building in Kansas City from Class C to Class B. The cap rate in that area went from 10 percent to 7 percent. After remodeling—at a total cost of $360,000—the rents went from $500 to $900 per unit. Assuming all expenses stay constant, let's consider how much I increased my property value by investing this $360,000.

VALUE = NOI / Cap Rate

VALUE

INCREASE = NOI Increase/Cap Rate

= (($900-$500) x 12 units x 12 months) / 7%

VALUE = $822,857

I spent $360,000 but increased my property value to $822,857. If I used $360,000 of my own cash, my rate of return on this would be 128 percent. Since I used the HELOC from my own home with a 4 percent interest rate, my monthly payment is $1,200. I only needed to rent out two units to cover this. Taking out HELOC of your own home can be risky, but it can pay off if you use it wisely to invest in an appreciating asset with proper analysis up front.

Let's use the same example to further understand why people invest in areas like the Bay Area despite such a low cap rate. Assume the twelve-unit building is in San Francisco, and I increased the same amount of NOI on the property. The only difference is the cap rate at 3 percent instead of 7 percent in Kansas City.

VALUE = NOI / Cap Rate

VALUE = (($900-$500) x 12 units x 12 months) / 3%

VALUE = $1,920,000

By investing in the Bay Area, you can double what you make in Kansas City! That's why most people who invest in low-cap-rate areas focus on building equity, not cash flow. If you do not need to use the cash flow to replace your income, you should have some real estate in a low-cap-rate area also.

RESIDENTIAL LOAN VERSUS COMMERCIAL LOAN

Financing for one-to-four-unit buildings falls under residential loan programs. Guidelines at different banks may vary, but typically, these loans require a 25 percent down payment, and you must qualify based on your personal credit and debt-to-income ratio (at approximately 40 to 45 percent). The income calculation includes your personal income plus 75 percent of the rental income from the property.

Financing for buildings with five units or more falls under a commercial loan program. These largely look at the NOI of the building rather than your income. These loan programs typically allow for a 80 percent loan to value or 1.25 Debt Service Coverage Ratio (DSCR)—whichever gives a lower loan amount. DSCR means the NOI has to be able to cover the mortgage payments by 1.25x.

DSCR = NOI ÷ Annual Mortgage Payments

Most commercial loan programs offer a twenty-five-year amortization program rather than a thirty-year amortization program like a residential loan product. The interest rate is fixed for a much shorter term compared to a regular thirty-year fixed-rate mortgage—ranging from three to ten years. There are also prepayment penalties on commercial loan products, whereas residential loans typically do not have any prepayment penalties. Lastly, residential loan programs usually limit an individual to have no more than ten residential loans on your personal credit reports. Commercial loan products, however, do not go on your personal credit and do not have limitations on the number of loans. There are many variations of commercial loan products, depending on your local bank or credit union, as well as government loan products.

Residential Loans versus Commercial Loans:

MOST COMMON	Residential Loan	Commercial Loan
Property Types	1-4 Units	5+ Units
Down Payment	25%	25% or 1.25+ DSCR
Qualification	Personal Credits	Property's NOI
	Personal Income	
	75% of Rental Income	
Fixed Rate	Up to 30 years option	Up to 10 years only
Amortization	0	Mostly 25, but some have 30
Prepayment Penalty	None	Yes
Loan Limits	Up to 10 loans on personal credit report	No limits
Credit Reports	Appears on personal credit report	Does not appear on personal credit report

KNOW THE POTENTIAL MISTAKES

Mistake 1: Underutilizing property equity. The worst mistake a person can make is squandering their home's equity or using their home equity on depreciating assets like fancy cars. If equity is just sitting there, then in many ways, your return on investment is essentially return on the equity. You must consider the opportunity costs. What could you have done with the equity? You have several options:

- You can invest in another cash flow property.

- You can use the money to reposition your current property.

- You can invest in trust deed notes.

Mistake 2: Another common real estate investment mistake is trying to get the best deal at the lowest cost. Though this sounds like an ideal scenario, if this is your standard, you won't ever buy anything. I have seen people miss out on opportunities over and over again because they wanted the best deal, the cheapest property, the lowest loan options, the hardest negotiation. They want to win big, but in the end, they lose big because they never take action.

Mistake 3: When it comes to real estate investment, don't make the mistake of having a short-term vision. Think ahead. Run the numbers. We utilize our CCIM ten-year analysis to help our clients plan their strategies for the property for the next decade. Maybe it's a dilapidated property now, but most things can stabilize in a few short years. Real estate allows you to have a clear picture and form solid strategies before you invest. Leave speculating for the stock market.

BEGIN WITH THE END IN MIND

When it comes to investing, put the numbers in front of you. When you can organize and analyze the numbers, you are making your real estate investment decisions with rationale, not with emotion. As I mentioned, even as an investor, I found it difficult to purchase my own home. All of my reasons to avoid buying were fear-based: Is this the right time? Did I overpay? This is why everyone benefits from an objective third party.

Rather than grapple with these subjective questions, when I plugged the numbers into a spreadsheet, I could make a decision based on objective fact, not subjective feelings. It becomes less about risk versus reward and more about the net income number. Real estate investing has a reputation of being risky, but if you use a formula to guide you, you alleviate much of the risk. Investment can be a science, but you have to begin with the end in mind.

> **YOU NEED TO VISUALIZE WHAT YOUR FUTURE IS GOING TO BE, AND THEN YOU CRAFT YOUR LIFE TOWARD THAT. YOUR MARKET ANALYSIS AND SPREADSHEETS ARE LIKE FINANCIAL DREAM BOARDS TO MAP OUT YOUR FINANCIAL FUTURE.**

As in all areas of life, planning and visualizing what you want in the future is a powerful way to make decisions. A sculptor doesn't just start haphazardly manipulating clay. He has an image clearly in mind, and each stroke and movement takes him one step closer to actualizing that vision. In the same way, you need to visualize what your future is going to be, and then you craft your life toward that. Your market analysis and spreadsheets are like financial dream boards to map out your financial future.

So many of us are short-term thinkers—ruminating about this hour, this day, this week, this month, this year. Most successful people think long-term and have five-year, ten-year, twenty-year plans. They're charting their courses toward success and financial freedom. I always make the first step with the end result in mind. I always have an end goal, and then I work backward from that.

I remember having the goal of a bank account with $10,000 in it. Since I had less than $100 in my account at the time, it seemed so far-fetched, but I doggedly pursued that goal, and I achieved it. I didn't let one hour pass without replacing that goal with a new one—$100,000, $200,000, $500,000, $1,000,000. I didn't just make the goal; I went back to the numbers and determined how many deals I would need to do a year, a month, in order to achieve those goals. How much passive income would I need to bring in to reach that goal? When I stepped back and looked at the numbers, they looked ridiculously large. I remember thinking, *Can I actually do this? Is it even possible?* Each time I reached a goal, the next one seemed too far-fetched. When I break it down into monthly objectives, however, it seemed doable. Because I started each morning with my end goal in mind, I eventually got there.

Make goals, keep your eye on them, and then work backward. This simple process keeps you on track and ever evolving. You don't get complacent or stagnant. You don't get distracted by other things if something goes wrong. You don't just give up the goal; you fix what went wrong so you can continue on the path. You keep pushing yourself toward excellence and raising the bar each time you achieve it.

Whether you are in real estate or not, this is a personal strategy that can reap exponential rewards for you and your family. If you feel content with your achievements, you stop improving yourself. Constantly cultivating yourself, your portfolio, your finances, your home, and your relationships is incredibly fulfilling. When I think back to what I had when I came to the United States and the family and business I've built, I feel so happy and grateful. I have all I ever wanted, but I still have goals that I will doggedly pursue. My ambitions have evolved as I've created more success for myself. Rather than being focused on my own financial future, I now have the goal of helping others reach their full potential. I will never be finished achieving. It's not about the dollar amount; it's about offering more people paths toward their own freedom and happiness.

ADVICE ON FINDING INVESTORS

If you don't have money for investing, you need to go find it. To be honest, finding money is the easiest part of real estate investing. It's finding the deals that are harder. If you find a deal but don't have the money, you could partner with a money investor. How do you convince this money investor to invest with you? You have to build an offering memorandum to convince them. The presentation needs to include a few key elements:

1. The property's location: Why did you choose this market, and how do you think the market will evolve? Explain why you chose the property. Use the market analysis spreadsheet to justify your choice. Too many people choose a market without understanding why.

2. The property's amenities: Is there public transportation? Keep in mind that if your property is in a low-income area, public transportation is even more important because tenants might not have cars. Are there grocery stores within walking distance?

APARTMENT INVESTING ANALYSIS

3. Potential development: I research the city planning to see if there is a projected path of development. If so, share the trends you foresee—how might they affect employment opportunities, rent, etc.

4. Plans for the property: What are your plans for the property in terms of rehab, raising income, decreasing expenses?

5. Your team: What property managers and contractors do you plan to use?

6. Property value and cash flow analysis: You need to create a clear picture of how you derived the property value and how you foresee the next ten years of cash flow.

7. Exit strategies: What are your exit strategies if it doesn't work out? Investors only have confidence in you if you have already thought of everything for them. Think about what the investor might ask you, and address it before they have the chance to ask. This is how you build confidence and competence.

8. Money: How much money do you need, and what are your expectations for returns? What are you offering the investors? You need to make it attractive enough for the investors to invest with you. What is the rate of return?

As I have learned countless times in my career, when it comes to real estate investing, getting money is the last thing you need to worry about. Don't forget, I was able to buy an apartment building using money I essentially found in my trash can. Find a deal first, and money will follow.

CONCLUSION

Through my life and career challenges, I have learned that I can deal with any obstacle by remembering that every problem has a solution. My passion for real estate never died, even when I was failing, even when I bought a property that was uninhabitable, even when we bought a home that we had to let go of. There were times I hid in a room and cried until I fell asleep, but I always knew I had more in me. I just didn't know when I'd become the person I wanted to be.

My whole life has been spent in pursuit of something:

- Finding a way back to my parents

- Finding my confidence as the "less pretty one," the "thicker one"

- Finding my cultural identity

- Finding a country that accepts me

- Finding a career that I am passionate about

- Finding financial security

- Finding my place as a minority female in a predominantly Caucasian, male-dominated industry

- Finding the man who will love and respect me

- Finding my place as a mom

- And perhaps the biggest pursuit of all: Finding my way home

As I look back, I'm thankful for the experiences I've shared within these pages. They have strengthened my faith, increased my stamina, and made me a more motivated and compassionate person. I have now found the elusive things I doggedly pursued for decades—I found financial security, a reunion with my parents, a successful real estate and speaking career, my place as a citizen of the United States with Chinese and Indonesian heritage, and a wonderful family.

Although my parents have regretted the struggles I have faced, I have thanked them for letting me go to find my own way home. It took me over twenty years, but when I look around at the life and career I have built for myself, I feel proud—proud of my challenges, proud of my mistakes, proud of my endurance. In my home and my career, I have found security and peace. Are there any greater rewards?

In sharing my own story, I hope to inspire you to take control of your life. Even if you have no resources, there are always opportunities—no matter your gender, skin color, financial status. It's up to you, however, to find them and grab hold of them. You can have it all. It's not easy, but it is possible.

Despite my disadvantages of being a woman in a male-dominated industry, being a minority, being an immigrant with a language barrier, being poor, being without resources or networks, I never let those be barriers to my own success. By staying focused on the major lessons shared in this book, you too can turn disadvantages into opportunities.

You need to have self-acceptance and self-confidence. Throughout my life, the one thing I struggled with the most was self-confidence. Over time, I learned that without it, I was paralyzed. No matter what your "labels" are—*immigrant, poor, minority, disabled*—don't let them be barriers to your own success. Accept yourself first, and then find your unique place in the world. When I'm interviewed, I'm often asked, "How does it feel to promote diversity in a Caucasian male-dominated industry?" My answer is always, "I think diversity comes from within, not from other people." I have a choice to be surrounded by people like me—Asians, mothers, women—but then I'm not practicing inclusion. Even though it might be uncomfortable (especially at first), when I surround myself with diversity, I encourage others to accept me. That's ultimately how I grew my confidence. I made myself uncomfortable until I became comfortable.

Use all your resources. When you use lack of money or resources as excuses, you are limiting your potential. Even if you have nothing—like I did when I came to the United States—you still have the valuable resources of time, intellect, and endurance. The less you start with, the more resourceful you need to be. Don't let certain criteria limit you.

Pace yourself. One of the main reasons people fail is because they want to run before they can walk. Life is a marathon, not a sprint. When you try to grow too fast, you become paralyzed. It may take years for your effort to be seen. You need to be well-informed with a clear goal before you proceed. Take baby steps and trust the process of growth and personal evolution. In whatever new endeavor you pursue, give yourself small, attainable goals. This is how I counsel new investors, and I have seen how breaking larger goals into smaller steps helps avoid burnout and feeling overwhelmed.

Stay focused on your "why." What is your objective? What is your goal? Why are you doing what you're doing? If you don't have a strong "why," you don't know what your end goal is. Your life is not going to change right away. If you are persistent, however, and you know what your end goal is, then by taking one step at a time, you will get there.

Maintain your ethical standards. Personal character is also a resource that's often overlooked. For me, ethics are a major component of my "why." As a working mom, some people might say I'm showing my children that money is more important than family. In fact, I'm teaching them the reason I work: to earn money to help others in hopes to make a difference in someone's life. I'm showing them, just as my mother, who became my idol, showed me.

Find your strengths and create your legacy. We all have strengths, so we all have *power*. Once we identify our strengths, we should use them to help others. I realized that real estate consulting was one of my strengths. Now I use it to help others achieve their financial security. Through this strength, I hope to change people's lives in a positive way and leave a legacy.

Though one of the benefits I've garnered from applying the above lessons is financial security, that is not the most valuable reward I have achieved. Through my own process of self-discovery, I have found confidence, happiness, and peace.

The true measure of success is happiness. Many people may have more than me, or had things come easier for them, but they aren't happy. I believe as long as I continue to be grateful for what I have, I'll be content. The only failure I fear is complacency. If I stop striving, then I stop thriving. I can be more successful, and I can make more money, but that doesn't mean I'll be better off. What's going to make me happier is knowing what my next goal is. I will continue achieving my goals and attempting to make our world better in the process.

If I didn't acknowledge the heartaches, the pain, and the struggle it took to get here, I would not fully appreciate my happiness today. I understand that many people might read this book seeking financial freedom, but I hope they find much more. I hope they see that life and contentment are oftentimes hard-won rewards for diligent work and perseverance. I hope they see that the first step to building anything—confidence, career, security—is taking action. I hope they see that no matter who they are or how far they've wandered, they can find their way back to themselves, to their peace, to their purpose, to their home. That's your *power* to change lives.

ACKNOWLEDGMENTS

In August 2018, when I was contacted by the Advantage|ForbesBooks team regarding my story, I thought it was a hoax. When I was offered the opportunity to write this book and to become the very first Asian Forbes Speaker, I knew I had to grab onto this opportunity to share my stories with the world.

Though I deeply believe my stories are the reason I became who I am today, I never thought those stories would draw interest from a book publisher. I did not believe I was capable of putting a book together while raising three young children, running my real estate businesses, and volunteering in numerous real estate organizations. However, after I met with the Advantage|ForbesBooks team in Charleston, South Carolina, my desire to fulfill this impossible dream became stronger than ever. I realized that this book could serve as a legacy for my children; a "Thank you" to my parents, who gave their all to me; and an expression of love to my husband, who stood by me through thick and thin. When I think bigger, I realize this book could potentially give someone the power to change their life by changing how they view their past. If this book can help just one stranger, then this is well worth my time and effort.

I have found my way home and achieved my goal of becoming financially independent, and I hope my stories will empower you even during difficult times and transform adversity into power to change your own life.

Every night, I pray with my children, and each of us shares our own gratitude for the day and what we need help with. Through this acknowledgment, I'd like to share my gratitude and ask for God's guidance.

To my three children, Matty, Nathan, and Lizzy: This book is written as a legacy and keepsake for you. Thank you for listening to my stories; now they are on paper. You are my most joyous achievements ever.

To my dad: I wouldn't have been able to write this book without you. You are my inspiration to develop good character every day.

To my mom: I have always wanted to become a woman like you. You are my role model. 入得厨房,出得厅堂. Thank you for being an amazing mother, wife, and businesswoman.

To my husband, John: Thank you for allowing me to flourish and pursue my passion. You never felt intimidated by my ambition; rather, you work with me as a team to raise our family while we each pursue our own goals in life. You made me feel confident about myself, which was what I lacked before I met you.

To my sister, Angelina: Thank you for taking care of Mom and Dad after I left Asia; you gave them a lot more than I could. I am glad that I can finally do the same.

To my brother- and parents-in-law: Thank you for accepting me for who I am and embracing me as part of your family.

To Susanna: Thank you for being my little sister, my best friend, and my partner who has been there for me during my ups and downs over the last thirty-six-plus years.

To my high school friends: Thank you, Rebecca and Eliza, for keeping me sane when I first moved to California.

To the NorCal CCIM Chapter leadership and members: Thank you for accepting me and giving me an opportunity to be your leader despite the fact that I don't fit the stereotypical chapter president profile.

To the HAYLEN team: Susanna Leung, Peter Whang, Anthony Wong, Trey Zhou, and Jose Monar—I am proud of our team; thank you for working together to elevate the real estate industry standard.

To my dearest friends and colleagues in the business:

Sanjeev Jaiswal: Thank you for your friendship and your generous heart for our family. You have been my business role model, and I am very grateful for having you in my life.

Winnie and Thomas Liu: Thank you for trusting me with your real estate investments and being my advocates! I am so touched by the close friendship we have built through the years.

Eric Rehn: Thank you for pushing me to write and put my stories into a book.

Andi Cummings: Thank you for making me a better leader.

Kevin Cole: Thank you for ensuring that I did not let go of the opportunity to join the ForbesSpeakers platform.

ABOUT THE AUTHOR

Helen Chong was eighteen years old, alone, and desperately trying to escape her family's financial struggles in Asia when she arrived in the United States for the first time. Before long, Helen had broken all stereotypes—as an immigrant, a minority, a woman, and a mom—on her path to becoming a successful entrepreneur specializing in real estate sales and investments. Now, she is the founder of HAYLEN Group, dedicated to elevating the real estate industry by focusing on high standard sales practices and helping her clients build their real estate portfolios, beginning with their first homes.

The struggles Helen's family faced during her childhood opened her eyes to how the loss of financial stability and the resulting loss of a home changed her family dynamic. What's more, after witnessing (and escaping) the ethnically driven riots in Indonesia that followed the 1998 Asian financial crisis, Helen understood how financial instability and struggle can affect society at large.

These experiences helped Helen survive in a foreign country, learn a new language and culture, fight against stereotypes, and build up the confidence to gain financial independence through real estate, one small step at a time.

Helen Chong is now a proud wife of a US marine veteran, John, and a mother of three children (Matthew, Nathaniel, and Elizabeth). Professionally, she is a top real estate producer leading her own team, an avid volunteer within the real estate industry, and an active real estate investor. In 2020, Helen served as the President of the Northern California Chapter of CCIM (Certified Commercial Investment Member) and she was nominated for the Industry Impact Award at ELEVATE, an event organized by the Registry and the Bay Area Commercial Real Estate for Women (CREW). Through speaking as a ForbesSpeaker, contributing business articles on Forbes.com, and authoring a biography about her experiences as an immigrant, a minority, a woman, and a mother, she hopes to inspire others who would like to break stereotypes and take control of their destiny.

HAYLEN SERVICES

elen Chong is the founder of HAYLEN Group, a residential and commercial real estate brokerage firm focusing on consultation and analysis to help their clients to build their real estate equity and/or portfolio.

HAYLEN GROUP OBJECTIVE

To inspire the public to become financially independent at retirement through real estate and to elevate the real estate industry standards with our high quality consultation services.

HAYLEN GROUP MISSION

To become the most highly sought real estate consultants, who help ordinary people achieve long-term financial security and independence by inspiring our clients with our expertise and high quality service, as well as treating them as if we were their partners.

Through her work with HAYLEN Group, Helen Chong is regularly interviewed for various webinars, podcasts, and publications. She also teaches how to perform in-depth real estate investment analysis at real estate organizations and investment clubs. Helen hosts numerous webinars, because she believes not only that education can help elevate the real estate industry's reputation, but also that it bridges the information gap between the industry and consumers. She focuses on helping others in the United States and Asia to improve their mindset, as she understands that mindset is the key factor in changing one's destiny to succeed.

LEARN MORE AT

Real Estate Brokerage www.HAYLENGroup.com/HG-TV
Speaking and Writing www.PowerToChangeLives.com
International Real Estate Education www.USPropertyDream.com
Messaging
Telegram: @HAYLENRealEstate
Facebook: @HAYLENGroup